T0065200

POST HOLE DIGGER

POST HOLE DIGGER

JAMES POPE

ARCHWAY
PUBLISHING

Archway Publishing books may be ordered through booksellers or by contacting:

Archway Publishing
1663 Liberty Drive
Bloomington, IN 47403
www.archwaypublishing.com
844-669-3957

Because of the dynamic nature of the Internet, any web addresses or links contained in this book may have changed since publication and may no longer be valid. The views expressed in this work are solely those of the author and do not necessarily reflect the views of the publisher, and the publisher hereby disclaims any responsibility for them.

Any people depicted in stock imagery provided by Getty Images are models, and such images are being used for illustrative purposes only. Certain stock imagery © Getty Images.

ISBN: 978-1-6657-5080-6 (sc)
ISBN: 978-1-6657-5079-0 (e)

Library of Congress Control Number: 2023918577

Print information available on the last page.

Archway Publishing rev. date: 09/28/2023

DEDICATION

Post Hole Digger is dedicated to the children of the world, like myself, that became instant adults shouldering family responsibilities far beyond our age.

I was 15 years old, in the 9th grade. My father died in my arms as I tried to get nitroglycerin tablets under dad's tongue. I took dad's job as janitor of the Macedonia, Iowa, consolidated school supporting my mother, older and younger sister.

CHAPTER ONE

Only a dim lantern light showed in the downstairs farmhouse window.

Raging blizzard and the icy blast of wind straight from Canada created huge snowdrifts in the Iowa farmyard and rattled the windows of the house. In the nearby barn, a mournful cow lowed.

The three little Pope girls were snuggled up in comforters in the upstairs bedroom. Jean, the oldest, was awakened by something. "Bonnie, is that you crying?"

Bonnie, her kid sister, woke up wiping her sleepy eyes. "Whaaat?" she mumbled. Jean turned to the youngest sister, Frances. "Franny, is that you?"

Franny too was awakened, sleepy-eyed. "No."

Jean said, "It's coming from downstairs. Does Dad have a new baby sheep downstairs by the stove?" They heard their father's voice at the bottom of the stairs. "No, it's not a lamb. It's your new baby brother. Come on down and meet him."

The girls thundered down the stairs. Bill was sitting by the stove holding a bundle. Grandma Della was at the stove, tending to towels in a tub of hot water. In the nearby bedroom, they saw their mother, Alice. She was watching.

The girls crept up to Dad to see. They crowded around eagerly to get the best look. Soon they were fussing over the baby, begging their father to hold him.

Bonnie said, "What's his name?' Dad said, "James Wilson Pope."

The girls started whining about who was going to hold him first. Grandma Dell hushed them up, saying, "Mom has to see the baby right now." The girls could see their mother, Alice, in bed in the next room. They followed Grandma into Mom's room and hovered around the baby who was now with his mother.

Back in the kitchen, Jean asked, "Why didn't you name him James Scott Pope after Grandma Pope's side of the family?"

Bill looked at the infant and simply said, "James Wilson, that's a good, stately Scottish name."

The next day about noon, Grandma called the girls into the kitchen to talk. They could tell by the tone of her voice that it was going to be one of those serious talks. Adults had a way of letting the kids know when something was important and required their attention.

When they were all seated around the kitchen table, Grandma spoke. She panned them around the table first, her blue eyes narrowing. "When your father was thirteen years old, his mother and father left their seven children with whoever would take them and ran off. They got divorced. Nobody ever heard from them again. That's why your mom and dad gave the baby the middle name of Wilson from our side of the family." The kids all gazed at Granny with respectful attention, but what she had said meant little to them, and they were soon dismissed to go about their morning.

It's sad going through life never knowing your grandparents. My uncle, Dad's brother, was working for the UP railroad. He went into a barbershop in Denver. He was stunned finding his mother was the barber. He told her, "You're not cutting my hair," and walked out.

CHAPTER
TWO

———

Bill and Alice were in the cornfield with a team and wagon. They were picking corn by hand. Bill, a medium-built man, and Alice, a portly, sturdy woman, was working along side him. A baby's cry from the wagon got Alice's attention. Got to tend to Jim. Bill stopped the team, and Alice climbed up on the wagon.

Bill asked, "What's wrong?" as Alice climbed into the wagon.

Soon she called back. "The ears of corn were bouncing off the bangboard, hitting him. I'll push some corn into that corner to raise him up."

Can you recall what your first memory was? Was it having fun playing with toys? Were you getting a bath? Was your father pushing you in a swing? Were you sad? A smile always creeps across my face as I recall that first memory. I once read a psychologist said that the only way a person changes his value system is through a significant emotional event. I sure don't know about value systems, but getting hit with ears of corn, the event was sure emotional. Welcome to the world, Jim.

By the time Jim was three, he was doing farm work. Everybody worked on the family farm. The kids were part of the labor force, which was the way most American farms operated.

Jim was helping his dad cleaning the furrowing pens and playing with the baby pigs when Jean found him. She said, "I got a plug of Dad's Days Work chewing tobacco. Let's find Tobacco."

After a quick search, they found their pet deer, Tobacco, down in the orchard. Jean broke off a corner of the chewing tobacco. "Here, Tobacco, it's your favorite."

The boy began to pet the deer. "Let me feed him."

"We have to be sure to save most for Dad. He'll be mad if he runs out."

As they headed back to the house, it started to rain, and they broke into a run. The deer raced ahead of them.

Jim, running, gasped, "I bet Tobacco beats us."

At the house, Tobacco was waiting on the front porch. He was barely breathing hard. When Jean opened the front door, Tobacco went in with them.

Alice approached and petted the deer. "Tobacco, you spoiled thing," she admonished. She reached in a bowl on the sideboard. "Here's your favorite candy." Soon all four kids were playing with the deer. When the rain stopped, the deer ran to the front door.

Bonnie said, "As usual. The rain stopped, and now Tobacco wants out."

Frances opened the door. The deer sprinted out and leaped off the porch in one graceful bound running across the yard.

One day when Jim was four, Jean was sweeping out the screened-in back porch.

Jim is about to get a lesson on being careless.

Jean, busily sweeping, heard her father's voice calling. He was running toward the house, carrying Jim. The girl called, "Mom, something happened to Jim!"

By the time Bill reached the house, Jim's screams of pain startled everyone. A panicky Alice called, "What happened?"

Panting, Bill said, "Jim was chasing cats in the haymow and fell through a hay throw-down hole!"

Alice immediately got on the phone while the girls tried to comfort Jim. In a minute, they heard Alice saying, "Okay, Doc Hayes, we'll be there as soon as we can."

Soon Dr. Hayes was announcing that Jim had broken his collarbone. "I'm going to have to put him in an upper-body cast."

Alice commented, "In this heat, he'll be miserable."

Dr. Hayes said, "If he gets to fussing bad, pour some cornstarch down inside the cast."

Jim was now five. Everyone was around the breakfast table. The boy's work of gathering eggs and feeding the chickens was about to be expanded.

Bill said, "Jim, today you can help me. I have to cut skids for a portable hog house. I need you on one end of the crosscut saw. Then I've got some dirt work to do. Do you think you can drive the horses while I handle the slip scraper?"

Jim was eager to do it. Soon they were moving dirt to fill in the ruts and holes. Jim was in his glory with the work and the responsibility.

One morning in the farmhouse, Jean took matters into her own hands and gave Jim a stern lesson in humility.

Alice was announcing to the kids, "Wash day. Bonnie, Frances, and Jim get all the dirty clothes and pile them on the floor on the back porch."

Jean pushed the washing machine closer to the door and uncoiled the exhaust hose out the door.

Jim came in carrying a load of clothes, dumping them on the floor, whining, "I hate that machine. It's loud. It fills the room with blue smoke and stinks up the whole house!"

Jean grabbed Jim by the arm and shook him. "Don't you say anything like that again! Mom hired out picking corn by hand to earn the money to buy it. You can wash your own clothes by hand. Pick out your clothes, and go out to the rain barrel and wash them."

By now Jim was sobbing from the dressing down.

Jean was not done. "Think about what Mom did for us, and say you're sorry for what you said." Jim, still weeping, sobbed, "I'm sorry."

"You're lucky Mom didn't hear you."

Around the dinner table, Alice was talking. "School year will soon be here. I guess we need to start getting things ready. Jim, you get to join your sisters this year."

On school day, Alice was seeing the kids off as they headed for school. She called, "Wait! Take these tin cans along. We have to do our part for the war effort. If you need to, you can stop at Ruby's."

Jim, complaining, said, "I can't walk that far."

Alice stood, hands on hips "Big strong boy like you? Your sisters did it, and they are girls. Why, it's only three miles each way."

Now in the past, Jim had watched each day as his sisters headed down the road toward town. However, he didn't realize just how far it was and how long it took to walk the three miles. Family friends, Earnest and Ruby Brinaman, lived halfway between the farm and the school. Rain, shine, or snow, the four walked the six miles each day. Once in a while, they would get a ride.

Bill and Alice were eating lunch. A dog, barking and growling, interrupted their conversation. Bill asked, "Whose dog is that?"

Bill and Alice rushed out the back door to see a stray dog attacking Tobacco. Bill yelled at the dog. The deer sprinted off, seemingly unharmed.

Alice said, "I hope Tobacco isn't hurt." "He ran like he's okay. He'll be back."

Bill and Alice were eating lunch. Alice said, "This year during corn-picking, let's do it different. Jean is old enough to help me cooking. Why don't you let Bonnie, Frances, and Jim throw off your last load of corn by hand so you can get started on chores sooner?"

Bill cocked his head as he munched on his lunch. "I don't know. That's a lot of work for the three of them."

Alice, pausing to think, said, "How many bushels are in a load?" "Fifty, maybe fifty-five."

"That's only about sixteen bushels each. They'll just be throwing it into the corncrib, not carrying it." Bill thought it over. "It sure would let me get the day's work done an hour sooner."

The children were coming in from school in their usual flurry. Mom was bustling about the kitchen, having expected them. "I know you're all starving. Here, I made some buns."

They happily tore into the snack, but little did the Pope kids know that they would soon be grieving for their beloved pet deer.

It was early evening, and everybody was in the house except Jim. In a while, he came in, his voice tense. "When I went to feed Tobacco, I couldn't find him!"

Bill's voice lowered when he said, "This afternoon a stray dog attacked Tobacco, and he ran off. I thought he would come back by now. He never misses feeding time."

But Tobacco never came back. He could be seen in the distance every now and then, but he would never come close. The fear instilled in him by the dog never left him.

Jim learned a new lesson. That was not to quit until the job was done.

Bill pulled a wagonload of corn alongside the corncrib and unhitched the team. "Okay, kids, it's all yours. Like we talked, I'll give you a penny a bushel."

It was in this endeavor that Jim learned a lesson.

As a member of the family, sometimes you just have to work without expectation or reward as there was never enough money to pay the kids. Even at a penny a bushel.

Alice's voice carried throughout the house. "Okay, kids, it's Saturday, and you all know what that means."

Jean, frowning, mumbled, "Clean the lamps!" Bonnie added to her lament. "And churn the butter!"

The girls, nonetheless, got busy. They covered the table with paper and brought all the lamps for cleaning and filling. Jim brought in the lanterns from the outbuildings, and Jean retrieved the gallon can of kerosene from the back porch. All four worked at cleaning and filling.

Having completed cleaning, Bonnie, Frances, and Jim returned them while Jean cleaned up.

All the kids returned to the kitchen, where Alice was holding a two-quart jar almost full of cream. She said, "Get your chairs in place."

The four dutifully sat in a circle facing one another. Mom said, "Who does the first twenty-five?"

Bonnie piped up. "The last time we did it, I was the last one." Alice said, "Okay, Fran, you start out."

Alice handed her the jar. Frances took the jar and started shaking it and counting till she got to twenty- five. Then she handed it to Jim, then Jean, then Bonnie. This went on until butter was formed. Alice then poured the buttermilk into a large glass. "There, Dad will enjoy this."

When Bill came home, he was in a good mood. "Let's hurry and get chores done so we can get to town."

Saturday was special as the kids got to go to town and get their treat.

After dinner, they piled into Dad's old yellow '29 Chevy. Soon they were pulling into town. All the kids began begging. "Can we have our treat now! Please, please, Daddy!"

"Why don't you and your mother walk around first and see who's all in town? I need to stop at the hardware store, and then I'll pick up your treat and meet you back at the car."

Alice and the kids went one way, and Bill went the other.

When Bill returned to the car, Alice and the kids were waiting. They eagerly gathered around as Dad unwrapped a candy bar on the hood of the car. With his pocketknife, he divided it into four pieces, giving one to each child.

One-fourth of a candy bar. That was their big Saturday-night treat.

Alice said, "I'll go down to Skinny's Meat Market and get some cheese and lunch meat to have when we get home."

Later that night, they were sitting around the table, eating sandwiches and listening to the battery- operated radio.

They had to be careful about the radio battery. It could only be used for a little while because batteries were expensive.

In the middle of the night, the family was awakened by an electrical storm. Lightning pitch forked across the dark sky, and thunder rumbled and growled with an occasional ear-splitting clap.

Later, Bill's yell rang out through the house. "Fire! The barn's on fire!"

The family dashed downstairs to the porch. Bill ran to the barn. During the lightning flashes, they could see their neighbor Frank running to them across the road. In the backlight of the burning barn, they could see Bill and Frank watching helplessly as the barn burned.

Later, with the barn in ashes, Bill and Frank trudged back into the house. They were all sooty and sweaty. Frank said, "Thank God we were able to get the horses and milk cows out!"

Alice, her voice low, asked, "Is there anything left?"

Bill frowned. "No. We did manage to save the saddle. Everything else is a total loss. But I'm pretty sure the insurance will cover building a new barn."

Later, the scene was one of activity as a crew of carpenters built a new barn. Jim was busy picking up small odd-size boards and blocks. Then he settled in the dirt to play with the blocks.

When the barn was complete, Bill was busy trying to get the horses into the new barn. One horse bulked, refusing to enter. He was pulling and cussing at the horse, but it whinnied, stood on its hind legs, pulled on the rope, and refused to go into the new barn.

The carpenters cleaning up the area were watching Bill and laughing. One called, "Hey, Bill, I thought you knew all about horses."

Red-faced and through tight teeth, Bill yelled, "If you think you can do any better, why don't you try?"

The carpenter had a small ball of string. Now I don't recall if he tied the string around the horse's upper teeth or lip. The carpenter then stepped out in front of the horse and gave a couple of soft tugs as he spoke to the horse, and the horse followed him into the barn.

Bill, now madder, just huffed.

Laughing, the carpenter said, "You heard about old dogs and new tricks, Bill?"

It was a very warm evening and a family night at home. Bill and Alice were sitting at the kitchen table, discussing finances, Jim playing with his blocks. Bonnie and Frances were playing a board game; Jean was reading.

Wiping her brow, Alice said, "It's too hot upstairs for the kids to sleep."

Bill said, "We'll do as we always do on hot nights like this. There must be a storm brewing for it to be this hot." He called to the kids. "Make your beds so you'll be between the front and back doors."

All six did as he suggested. Bill said, "Maybe we'll be lucky, and a cross-draft breeze will blow up."

In the middle of the night, all six restlessly tried to sleep. When a cool breeze drifted through the house, Bill said, "Ma, you awake?"

"Yeah, I can't get to sleep."

"Feel that cool breeze. It must be coming through the rain. Breeze gets cooler. It must be coming off hail to be this cool." Just then a crack of thunder reverberated through the house. Then the lightning lit up the house. The air got even cooler as lightning bolts flashed against the sky. Then rain began, and the clatter of hail on the roof followed. Bill got up and went to the back porch. He paused and went back and lay down. The family was awake now.

Bill said, "Let it storm. Thanks to this cool breeze, we can all go back to sleep."

Early in the morning, Bill, milk buckets in hand, headed for the barn. Opening the top half of the walk-in barn door, he reached inside to unlatch the bottom half. He jerked his hand back and looked at the wood splinter in it. Inside the barn, Bill traced the track of wood splinters. Surprised and loose-jawed, he mumbled, "Who says lightning doesn't strike twice in the same place?"

Bill went back in the house with the two buckets of milk and set them down by the milk separator. He called for Alice. When she came in, she asked, "What's wrong?"

"Lightning struck the new barn!"

Alice too was slack-jawed at the revelation. "But that's why we had lightning rods put on the new barn."

"We were lucky the barn was still empty, no hay or straw, or it would've caught fire."

Summer turned to fall, and everyone helped pick the last of the last apples. As the apples were sorted, the very best ones were set aside for storage and the rest for canning. As the weather got cooler, the upstairs northwest bedroom had no heat to it, and it was turned into a cold storage room. The very best apples were polished, wrapped up in paper, and placed in the room. All the family members helped making an abundance of popcorn balls, candies, and cookies for the storeroom. During winter snowstorms, we always had unexpected gust. Stranded travelers getting stuck, come knocking. Some had to stay a day or two. Mom would motion to us kids, and we would follow her upstairs and fill pans and bowls with goodies. Our unexpected gusts were amazed. Dad would harness a team and pull the car off the road into the yard.

We had a pet goat that would race any car to the yard that turned into our driveway. If it was our car, the goat would race it to the garage. Our outdoor toilet was built onto the back side of the garage. You could enter from either the outside or from the inside of the garage. The goat would race into the garage and jump on the toilet seat. My uncle came to the farm. The goat jumped up on top of the car and fell through the cloth top and chewed up the seats.

There was a family meeting involving Bill and Alice and her folks, Della and her husband, Stuart.

Alice was frustrated. "But, Mom, we've been over this again and again. There is no money to buy you out!"

Della was fuming. "When your dad died, the law just is not fair giving the child two-thirds of everything and the wife only gets one-third."

Bill added, "We'll need all the extra money there is to switch from horse farming to modern equipment."

Della's voice was now petulant. "Well, Stuart and I aren't getting anything from this farm but some eggs and butter and garden stuff. We can't live on that. Your poor stepfather and I aren't getting any younger. We've decided to move to Seattle where there's a lot of work in the shipyard. We still have enough years to earn a good retirement."

Bill said, "If we took out a loan to buy you out, we wouldn't be able to pay it back. We'll lose the farm and still owe money."

Getting up, Della yelled, "I demand my share in cash now!" Then she and her husband stormed out of the house, got in their car, and left.

Later that evening, Bill and Alice were in bed. Alice said, "I just don't know what to do about Mom!"

"I know this farm has been in your family for a couple of generations, and it means a lot to you. But in this day and age, it is so small. Even if we had modern equipment, I don't know if we'd make enough money to pay for it."

Alice shook her head adamantly. "No! I won't stand for us to go into debt without some reasonable assurance we can come out ahead."

Later, when Bill arrived home from a trip into town, he met Alice in the front yard. She asked, "Any ideas?"

"Yes, but I'm almost afraid to say it." Alice said, "Let's hear it."

Scratching his head, Bill began to talk. "Well, I talked to a man in town that has a farm, and he wants to farm it on the shares. He has all modern equipment. He'd furnish everything, and I'd furnish the labor.

We'd split, him getting three-fifths, and we'd get two-fifths." Alice stood silent but thinking.

The next day she walked out across the field where Bill was working. Seeing her coming, he stopped what he was doing.

She said, "Bill, I've been doing a lot of soul-searching, and I have come to the conclusion that we should sell the farm and move on."

"I'm so sorry we couldn't make a go of it," he replied. "The farm's been in your family for a couple of generations. I know it hurts."

Later after breakfast the next day, they gathered the family together. Alice said, "Kids, it's time for a family meeting."

Jean asked, "Are you going to have a baby?"

Alice, rolling her eyes, said, "No. We're going to sell the farm and move."

The kids were aghast at the news. They began hammering questions in a rapid-fire way. "Where will be live? What will we do? Where are we going?"

Bill jumped in. "Look, kids, your grandmother needs some money for her and Grandpa Stuart to move to Seattle and start a new life. She well deserves it. We can't afford to pay off a loan to buy her share of the farm."

Alice said, "Your father has found a farm east of town. We think that will also give us a fresh start."

Bill added, "One thing in your kids' favor, you'll only have to walk a quarter mile to school. But it will be a country school. And another thing, everybody east of town will be getting electricity before this side gets it."

The girls shouted with joy. "Yaaay! No more smelly lamps and kerosene. No more Saturday cleanings." Bill said, "Hold on. The electricity won't happen for a while."

CHAPTER THREE

The new boss was showing Bill how to operate the Ford tractor and its equipment, familiarizing, Bill with everything.

Later at lunch, Alice said to Bill, "Can you drive me to town to pick up a few things?" "Sure, and I can pick up a couple of sacks of chicken feed at the elevator."

On the way, they stopped at the elevator truck scales. Bill said, "Wait here. I'll just run and order what I need then drop you off at the grocery store. While you're shopping, I'll come back and get the feed."

Alice completed her shopping and got back in the car. Looking around, she asked Bill, "Where's the feed?"

He said, "Grinder's broke. We've got enough feed for a few more days."

Late that afternoon, Alice was in the kitchen when the phone rang. It was her mother, Della. Della had a funny sound to her voice. "Hi Alice, heard any good news?"

Alice, puzzled, asked, "News? What news?" "I just found out you weigh 350 pounds."

There was a silence on the phone line. Finally, Alice said, "Three hundred and fifty pounds? What are you talking about?"

"It's all over town that you weigh 350 pounds. While the car was on the scales at the elevator with you in it, Bill went inside. The car was weighed. Then when Bill came back, the car was weighed without you in it. The elevator guys couldn't wait to spread the news."

Alice's voice went into a shriek. "That son of a bitch did that to me! Let me get my hands on him." She went running out of the house yelling for Bill.

Soon they were arguing. Bill claimed, "Honest, Mom, I didn't know anything about it."

Now I don't know what Mom said to Dad, but Dad slept on a day-bed in the living room for a while.

A few months later, little sister Mary was born. She and Mom slept in my upstairs bedroom; Dad and I slept in the downstairs bedroom. From that time on, Mom and Dad grew further and further apart.

One Sunday afternoon, Bill, Grandpa Stuart, and Jim were sitting on the porch. Grandpa Stuart said, "Bill, you feel lucky today?"

Without hesitating, Bill said, "I think we can even things up today." "You do the nailing. I'll get the rifles."

With a few taps of a hammer, Bill drove a nail partway into a garden post just deep enough to hold it. Stuart entered the porch from the house, carrying two rifles, and handed Bill his single-shot .22.

Bill took it and said, "You're one up on me, so you take the first shot." They then took turns firing at the nail, trying to drive it home.

Bill and Stuart were doing some friendly jawing back and forth as they continued to shoot at the nail. Bill's next shot drove the nail into the post.

Laughing, Bill said, "There, take that. That makes us even." Stuart grinned. "I don't think it's all the way in. I'll take a look."

He walked over and examined the nail. Then he turned to Bill. "Okay, I guess you win."

Back on the back porch, Stuart turned to Jim. "Son, I think it's time you learned to shoot." He then handed him the Springfield .22 semi-automatic rifle, and Jim handled it gingerly, looking at it in awe. Then Stuart began his instruction. "First thing you want to remember is, never point a gun at anything you don't want to shoot. Always make sure the weapon is unloaded before you put it away." He looked at Jim. "Any questions?" Jim shook his head. Then Stuart said, "Why don't you see if you can hit that knot in the post over there."

Jim picked up the rifle, sighted it carefully, and fired. He missed the post entirely.

Stuart said, "The gun is too heavy for you. Here, place it across the porch railing." Jim did it, and his next shot hit the post. He turned to the others, grinning broadly.

The family was at the supper table when Bill announced, "This Saturday, and we all have to work for the war effort. All the kids in our section will pick milkweed pods and carry them to school. All the men will be cutting hemp weeds. Our farm will be the collection site."

A curious Jim asked, "How can weeds help with the war?"

Bill had the answer. "The navy uses the silk from the pods for life jackets, and the hemp is used to make rope."

Later on, the men with tractors and hay wagons unloaded bundles of hemp, and the kids carried sacks of milkweed pods to the schoolhouse.

The family was at the train station to see Grandma and Grandpa off. Alice, wiping a tear said, "We'll surely miss you. All the things you did for us. Our holidays just won't be same."

Grandpa hugged the kids one by one. "I'll miss the fun times we had. When you're a little older, maybe we can help you come to Seattle."

Bill turned philosophical. "Do you have any regrets with your decision to move?"

Grandma said, "Not at all. We have plenty of money to buy a house and enough for us to live on for six months."

Grandpa chimed in, "And I have a job waiting for me at the Bremerton Naval Shipyard." The conductor called, "All board!"

There were hurried final hugs and kisses. The old folks boarded the train, and the family paused to watch the train pull away from the station. They watched till it was out of sight before turning sadly and leaving. A part of their life had gone.

CHAPTER
FOUR

The family was working in a large garden, busy planting. Alice said, "Bill, do you think the garden is large enough?"

Sizing it up, Bill said, "It's bigger than we've ever had."

"The family is getting bigger and eating more. We'll need a hundred quarts of all the major vegetables." At the supper table that night, Alice said, "After supper, we all need to go to the garden. Weeds will take over if we don't keep ahead of them."

On a hot summer day, Alice and the four kids were canning. There was a fire in the cook stove and tubs of boiling water on top of it. Frances and Jim were shucking sweet corn. Alice, Jean, and Bonnie were cutting corn off the cob. Corn milk was spattering all over.

Now the air was thick with flies. Alice propped the rear screen door open. "Okay, places, everyone!" All grabbed towels and headed for the far corners of the house. Waving their towels and arms, they shooed the flies out the back door. Alice slammed the door shut. "Don't know how to keep 'em out. We just keep repeating."

As they worked at the canning, Alice called to Jim. "We need more jar lids and sealing rubbers, Jim. You'll have to run to town. I'll call the grocery store and tell them what I need."

Jim set out at a trot for the two-mile run to town.

At the store, the grocer said, "Jim, you must be pooped. Here, take this bottle of pop."

Jim hesitated but, at the grocer's urging, took it. He almost emptied the bottle in one long swig.

The next day, they were still canning. Jim was wiping away tears as he cranked the hand grinder while shoving horseradish roots into it. "Mom, why is it always me that has to grind the horseradish?"

With a veiled grin, Alice said, "You're lucky that we only need a few pints and not the hundred quarts." It was a hot summer day, and Alice and Jean were working in the kitchen. Bonnie and Frances were on the back porch, washing clothes. Jim was out in the yard, pulling weeds. Little Mary's wail came from the upstairs bedroom.

Alice called Jim. "Jim, come in here and take care of Mary."

Jim went into the bedroom and picked Mary up from her crib, comforting her. Then he carried her into the living room to the open window and sat on the sill, holding her. As he rocked her back and forth, he lost his balance and fell backward out the window. He screamed, "Help! Help!"

Alice and the girls came running and looked out the window. Below, Jim was lying in the middle of a big thorny rosebush, Mary on top of him. The girls dashed out and helped them out of the bush.

Alice called, "Is Mary okay?"

Jean, inspecting her, said, "She must be fine, Mom. She's laughing." "How is Jim?"

Jim was wincing in pain. "Pull those thorns out," he wailed. Alice called, "Frances, get the iodine."

In the farmyard machine shed, Bill and Jim were looking over the Ford tractor and modern machinery. Bill said, "Thrashing time is still a long ways off, but this would be a good time for you to jump on your pony and ask the neighbors in our thrashing ring if you could haul water in to the bundle pitchers in the field."

Jim asked, "How much should I ask for?" "Two dollars a day."

Jim rode off on his pony to make his deal. Soon he was negotiating with his neighbors and started home by late afternoon.

When he arrived, Bill asked, "How did you do?" "Got five jobs."

"Good. When we get closer to thrashing time, we'll cover some jugs with burlap." "Why?"

"Helps keep the water cooler, and if you happen to knock them together, it'll help protect them. We'll cover four 'cause one always gets broken." He paused. "By the way, Mrs. Williams called. She wants you to weed her garden tomorrow. The walk is just a little further than the grocery store."

Next day, a sweating Jim finished in Mrs. William's garden. As she was paying him, she said, "That was a very good job you did. Here's four dollars. I'll call your mom when I need you again."

Jim stopped at the grocery store on the way home. He told the clerk, "I want fourteen candy bars and a bottle of pop."

"That'll cost a lot of money."

Jim pulled out a dollar bill and proudly handed it to the clerk. "That leaves you a lot of change. Do you want to buy more?" "No. I'll just save the rest."

Doing things like this gave Jim an enormous amount of pride. He liked the ability to earn and spend how he wanted.

At dinner that night, after everyone was seated, Jim walked around the table and placed two candy bars on each plate. There was a joyous outburst of gratitude.

Bill, smiling, said, "Jim, that was very generous of you, thinking of your family." Jim liked this kind of admiration from his parents too. It made him feel very grown-up.

Alice announced, "Okay, everybody. Save a half of a candy bar for later on this evening when we listen to the radio. We'll save the other candy bar."

After dinner, they were still at the table, when Bill said, "I talked to Jim Scott today. He wanted to know if anything good was growing in the timber. I told him blackberries, gooseberries, mushrooms, and tons of black walnuts. He and his wife and granddaughter are coming out Saturday."

Alice blurted, "Great. I haven't seen them in a long time."

Jim couldn't understand his mother 's excitement. After all, his grandmother was a Scott. A Scott child was the first white child born in this county.

On Saturday, Jim spotted the team and wagon turn into the long driveway. He didn't recognize them, and they got closer; he saw that their skin was black. He'd only learned about black people in school but had never seen any. He stayed out of sight and watched as his parents greeted them as old friends.

Alice called to the children, "Come and meet Mr. and Mrs. Scott and their granddaughter Sylvia."

All four children got a quick education on black people never having met any before. The kids were shy and standoffish as Mom introduced them. She said, "This is Jean, Frances, Bonnie, and Jim."

Later, Bill said, "If you got everything you need, we'll all get in your wagon and head for the timber." Soon all the kids felt comfortable, and all were visiting. Bill guided Jim Scott to the places to do the picking.

Jim took Sylvia aside. "Sylvia, I know some neat places to play." Sylvia asked her mom. "Mom, is it okay?"

"Yes, but don't go too far. We'll be moving all around the timber."

That afternoon back at the house, Alice and Mrs. Scott set about fixing something to eat.

Mr. and Mrs. Scott and Sylvia made several trips to the farm. Sylvia and Jim would go off riding his pony and exploring.

Jim hadn't known that there was a black family in town. Sylvia was his first playmate. When Jim was in the 3rd grade the Pope family moved to another town. Jim never saw Sylvia again. He had friends who remembered her as being in their town school class for a short period. He was told while her grandparents stayed in Avoca, she left to stay with relatives in Chicago or New York. Mr. and Mrs. Scott lived in Avoca until their deaths.

Jim's cousin Tuffy Pope's wife Karen, babysat for Sylvia in the sixties when she came back for her mother's funereal. I've thought about her a lot over the years and would like to know how she fared in life.

CHAPTER
FIVE

The power company started setting poles out from town. We kept track of the daily progress. It was a major event as the power poles were set past our farm. Jim was fascinated watching the power company set poles and stringing wire.

When the power company truck pulled in their driveway, Bill went out to meet them. After they left, Bill came into the house. "Mom, the power company will be here tomorrow to wire the house and outbuildings." The kids jumped with joy.

Jim and the girls watched, still fascinated, the next day as the power company men went about hooking their farm up to the modern age.

In the one-room country schoolhouse, the kids were eagerly listening to one of the kids that lived closer to town, telling about getting electricity. A few days later, as we came into the house from school, Alice walked to the new wall switch and sang out "Ta-da" as she flipped the switch and the bare light bulb in the kitchen ceiling lit up. We all stood and gazed in amazement, which turned into shouts of joy. Alice warned, "Not so fast, kids. We don't know how reliable this new electrical stuff is, so won't put the lanterns and lamps away yet."

The new technology, like all other technology, was suspect to rural people.

The Pope kids were in the habit of reporting anything and everything immediately to their parents. When they came in from school one day, Bonnie led off. "Mom, we learned a new way to say the Pledge of Allegiance to the flag today."

Frances added, "We can no longer hold our arm out, palm up, and point to the flag. It's too much like the Germans' Heil Hitler."

Alice folded her arms and said, "Can you believe that! Win or lose, Hitler changed us."

A stock truck drove up the long driveway. Bill and the driver had a long talk, and then the truck left. Jim, the most curious, asked his father, "Who was that?"

"Marvin Schlicht. I just got us a job. I rented him pasture ground for his horse, and he'll pay us to break the ones that need it and the colts. After I break the horses, you and I will tame them down to ride double and be gentle enough for kids to ride. And I'll help you break the colts. One of them is pretty special. His father is Roy Rogers's horse, Trigger."

Jim was awed. "Wow! Trigger."

Breaking horses was done much like the cowboys of the Old West did it. Bill roped a horse and made it run around the lot several times. He then pulled it close to a snubbing post, wrapped the rope around the post and handed the rope to Jim, and then Bill managed to get a saddle on the animal to mount it. That was no easy task since the horse resisted mightily. When he got on, Bill called, "Let him loose."

The horse danced on all fours and bucked and tried his best to throw Bill off. This went on until the horse, exhausted, gave up and submitted to the rider on his back.

Jim was busting to try it himself. Bill held a colt close to the snubbing post and helped Jim mount it. The colt jumped and bucked whinnying and running around, trying to throw Jim of, which it did. Finally, the colt, exhausted, stopped. Jim sat there triumphant as Dad called out, "Okay, that's enough for today, little buckaroo. You did a good job."

A few days later, Marvin's wife came driving up the lane. She said to Bill, "I'll be loading the horse to sell. Marvin got picked up for horse stealing in Oklahoma, and I need the money to pay the lawyer."

"Stealing horses?" Bill was flabbergasted. "Marvin? How'd that happen, and how did he get caught at it?"

"It's all a misunderstanding. As you know, Marvin is a trucker, and he can get all the gas rationing stamps he wants. He was in Oklahoma using out-of-state gas stamps. The Oklahoma Highway Patrol discovered where he last purchased gas and figured where his next gas stop would be."

"Did you know what he was doing?"

"No, not really. I thought it was just minor stuff, nothing big."

Marvin served four and a half years in the Oklahoma State prison.

When Bill went to load the horses, he had trouble. Trigger's colt refused to get in the truck. No matter what they did, the colt dug in his heels and, mule-like, refused to get in. Jim said, "Dad, see, Trigger Junior likes me and the farm so much he doesn't want to leave."

While the town kids were going to the movies watching Roy and Gene round up the bad guys, Jim was living it.

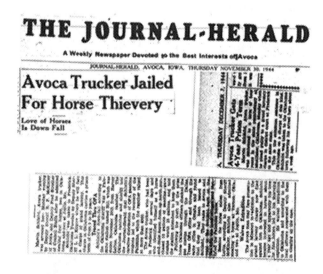

Jim yearned to get aboard another farm icon, and that was the tractor. In the farmyard, Bill and Jim stood looking at the Ford tractor.

Bill said, "Jim, you're big enough to learn how to drive the tractor. Get up in the seat. See how it feels. Take a look at the pedals and the controls and the gear shift."

Jim eagerly climbed up. "Now," Bill said, "to start the tractor, the first thing you need to do is have your foot on the brake. Make sure the tractor is out of gear. If the motor is warm, give it a little gas, and push the starter button."

Bill let Jim start the tractor several times till he got the hang of it.

"Now," Bill said, precisely, "look down here at the gear shift, and see the shift pattern. Start the engine, push down on the clutch, and put it in first gear, and give it a little gas." Jim did it with no trouble. "Good, now let up on the clutch slowly and smoothly." Inevitably, the tractor lurched forward.

Bill ordered, "Push down on the clutch and the brake." Jim did, and the tractor stopped.

"Now turn off the motor. Now start the tractor and move it." They practiced this over and over.

Bill said, "Now try driving it down to the end of the lane, and we'll do some gear changing." After a halting start, Jim mastered the operation.

Finally, Bill announced, "Okay, Jim, now that you know how to drive the tractor, you can feed the sheep while I do the other chores."

Jim was eager. Pulling a two-wheeled trailer behind the tractor, he drove into the alleyway of the corncrib. He opened a chute, letting a few bushels of feed pour into the trailer. He then drove into the sheep lot and scooped feed into the feed bunk.

Jim Pope on the FORD tractor, the first tractor I learned to drive. I was in the 3rd grade at New Boston #5 country school. We lived a mile and a quarter east of Avoca, Iowa. In My story I was driving as described on page 26.

Country school was fun. The teacher only had to have two years of college.

New Boston #5 Students of 1944.
Front row: Jim Cary, Ann Christy Gronborg, Richard Bolton
Middle row: Patty Allen, James Pope, Ilamae Camenisch, Darlene Camenisch
Back row: Bonnie Pope, Lyle Katle, Charles Allen, Frances Pope

During recess and at noon, she would join us playing games. There was a creek running past one side of the school yard. In the winter during noon recess, we played on the ice. The teacher would join us. She would check her watch and announce, "Okay, back to the school." We would always beg, "Just a little longer." She'd say, "Okay, just five more minutes." One time she made me stay after school, and she gave me a ride partway home. As she shifted gears, her dress was pushed up above her knee. My eyes were fixed on it. She quickly pulled the dress down.

In the winter after Dad had finished morning chores, he'd go to the school and start and start a fire in the big potbelly stove and carry in enough coal and wood to last the day. There was a herd of forty or fifty head of deer in our timber. Dad shot one, but when Mom cooked the meat, it tasted horrible. Someone told Dad to can it half and half with pork sausage. We all loved it with the rich gravy. For our school lunch in the winter, Mom would give us a quart jar of the deer-sausage mixture and a potato. At first recess, one of my sisters would loosen the lid and put the jar in a pan of water on the heating stove along with the potato. A wonderful aroma filled the room. At noon, we put a pie tin on our desk, split open the potato, and poured the deer/sausage mixture over it.

During that winter, all of us kids got the mumps. Our family was quarantined, and the county health office posted a big sign at the end of the driveway. Mom would call in an order to the grocery store, and items would be left at the end of the driveway.

Spring arrived. Bill said, "The tractor isn't heavy enough and loses too much traction when you plow with it. We'll take it to town and have fluid put in the tires."

Later at Holtz's garage in town, fluid was pumped into the rear tires.

Jim and his dad had a few things to learn about fluid in the tires. When going downhill, it was common practice to kick the tractor out of gear and let it coast, picking up speed.

Jim, driving the tractor by himself, was approaching the top of a hill. Just over the crest of the hill, he kicked it out of gear. As the tractor picked up speed, the centrifugal force made the fluid in the tires go around with the wheel. This didn't happen to both wheels at the same time, causing the tractor to jerk violently back and forth. Jim was able to get the tractor slowed down and under control.

Jim drove the tractor up the lane and stopped it by the machine shed. He said to his father, "Dad, don't kick the tractor out of gear going downhill. That fluid in the tires about jerked me off the road."

Bill scratched his head. "I didn't know it would do that. You sure taught me something."

Bill was mowing hay, and he scared a doe deer, and she ran away. As he got closer to where she was lying, he saw a fawn. The doe never returned to the fawn, and at the end of the day, Dad and I brought the fawn to the barn and made a pen. Everyone in the family tended to the fawn, and with cows' milk and good feed, it gained weight. Now I don't know if it was us kids talking about the fawn, but a neighbor turned us in to the game warden, who came and took the fawn away.

Another day in the farmyard, Alice was talking to Bill about Jim working at odd jobs off the farm. Bill retorted by saying, "I'll tell Jim. He'll like earning some extra money."

Jim got all kinds of extra work. Bill told him, "Jim, Mr. Carley wants to hire you to walk beans. It'll take you a couple of days. His wife will pick you up in the morning and bring you home at night."

"Great."

One day after finishing breakfast, Bill said, "Mom, I'm going into town and ride down to Macedonia with Uncle Young [Young Royal, real name], to look at the big show farm he works on. He lives in a trailer at the farm and keeps telling me how great it is."

Jim, Bonnie, and Frances, coming home from school, stormed into the house. As usual, Jim said, "Mom, I'm starved."

"Go change your clothes. I'll fix you a sandwich before you go do your chores." When Jim returned, he asked, "What's for dinner?"

"Jowls and turnip greens."

Jim's face twisted in distaste. Disgruntled, he said, "I'd rather eat pig shit than that stuff!" Alice said, "Here's your sandwich. I'll see if I can find something you like better for supper."

Little did Jim know he would soon have a strong emotional experience that would change his value system.

Jim was at the granary filling his pull wagon with chicken feed when Dad appeared. "Still have enough feed?"

Jim said, "I guess, enough for two or three more days."

"We need more feed for the milk cows too. I'll call the grinder tonight. By the way, what's Mom fix' n for dinner tonight?"

"Hog jowls and turnip greens. I told her I'd rather eat pig shit. So she said she'd find something I liked."

Bill was taken aback. "Jim, I think you owe Mom an apology. All she can fix is what we have. She doesn't have any control over what food is at hand."

That night at the dinner table, all except Jim were seated. Alice called to Jim, who was still outside. "Jim, dinner is on the table."

Jim rushed in and sat in his chair. His sisters, heads low, were snickering, holding back giggles.

Jim looked down at his plate. Wide-eyed, loose-jawed, he couldn't believe what he saw. There were two pig turds on it.

Bill, grinning, said, "The rest of the family thought you should have your favorite meal." Jim was in near tears. His sisters burst out laughing.

Bill said, "You can ask to be excused, go to bed, and think about what happened. In the morning, if you apologize to your mother and eat what she fixes you, you can eat with the family. If not, after we're done eating, you can fix yourself something and eat by yourself."

Later, after the kids were in bed, Alice and Bill were relaxing in the living room. Alice was thoughtful. She got up and said, "I think I'll go up and get Jim and fix him something."

Bill frowned and rolled his eyes. "You'll do no such thing. He's getting just a little too big for his britches. Just because he drives the tractor and does farm work, he thinks he's a man. This will be a good lesson for him."

Jim is the first one in the kitchen in the morning. His eyes full, he rushed into his mother's arms. "I'm sorry, Mom. I'm sorry."

That changed Jim's eating habits for life. Whether it be a peanut-butter sandwich or a lobster dinner, it was all the same, just food.

It was the last day of school. The kids were exuberant. Even the weather agreed, a bright, sunny, spring day in the countryside. Bonnie, Frances, and Jim, barefoot and wearing T-shirts, headed off to school, a bounce in their step.

Last day of school meant going off to the timber next to the school yard for a picnic. But by midmorning, the weather did an Iowa special. It turned cold and started snowing. By noon, six inches of snow covered the ground.

At the farm, Bill looked out the window, shook his head, and went out and hitched up the team to a bobsled. He packed it with warm clothes and shoes for the kids. For the Pope kids, it was a joyful, fun ride home bundled in the warm winter wear.

CHAPTER SIX

A few days later, Bill and Alice were standing in the yard, talking. Bill was raving about the experimental farm. "Mom, that farm down at Macedonia is sure something. Four hundred and eighty acres, nine tractors, and three Allis Chalmers Caterpillars. Uncle Young lives in a trailer on the farm, and every day four or five hired men drive down from Avoca."

"Does it have electricity?"

"Not yet, but they'll be getting it pretty soon."

Mom's brows furrowed as they always did when she had something important to think about. "Bill, I don't think we should move. We're just getting a little ahead. This is our hometown."

"Yeah, but we still have to hire someone to do custom field work. Our landlord doesn't seem too enthused about getting a bigger tractor and machinery. Down at Donia, that hobby farm has all the machinery you need. I still figure we'd be further ahead with me working by the month."

Alice lowered her head. "Let's sleep on it, and tomorrow we'll talk more."

The next day, Alice found Bill in the barn. She got his attention and then hesitated. "As much as I hate to say this, if you're sure you will get the job, I'll go along with moving."

Bill's smile gratified both of them.

Bonnie was walking up the lane from the mailbox, a letter in hand. As she got closer, she called, "Mom, we got a letter from Grandma."

Alice called all the kids to the kitchen. They were excited and curious about the letter.

Alice read it and then turned to the anxious children. "Well, she says they bought a house. Grandpa has a great job at the naval shipyard, and he's shipping us a big salmon fish packed in dry ice. Should arrive at the depot in about a week."

The kids had got wind of the move. Jean asked, "Mom and Dad, how big is the town of Macedonia? Does it have lots of stores?"

Bill grinned. "It ain't Chicago, but I checked the population. It's two hundred and thirty. When we hit town, it'll be two hundred and thirty seven."

With the decision made, it was time to auction off the stock and equipment. Bill stood silent during the auction process. His face dropped as the livestock was sold. He lowered his head and walked away at that point. Bill was a sensitive man and, unlike some, loved animals.

Moving to the new farm, Bonnie, Frances, and Jean complained as they unpacked the hated lamps and lanterns. Jean said, "I thought we were done with these things."

Bill shook his head. "For a while at least, it's back to doing chores in the dark. Electricity will be along soon."

In the new farmyard, Bill was teaching Jim how to use the new farm machinery. Jim was eagerly looking at one of the Caterpillars. "Dad, when can I learn to operate one of the Cats?"

"Hell, Jim, I don't even know how to operate them yet."

But soon Jim was bragging on his new life and all he had learned. "Boy, we ride a school bus, and we have electricity, and I can operate all nine tractors."

Bill grinned. "Now that you're hiring out doing tractor work, I'll call you Big Bucks. Sure, it's better than making fences and walking corn and bean fields. But you sure get tired sitting on the tractor all day."

Jim didn't think it was so tiring. He was thrilled by the idea of driving any machine.

At the breakfast table in the morning, Alice told Bill, "I need Jim to go to the corner store for me." Bill cocked his head. "Okay. He can use the Farmall C."

"Good. Then I'll call in my order. Bonnie, you ride along to help with the groceries."

Jim and Bonnie were rolling down the road. Jim, of course, felt extra big being the driver and his older sister the passenger. Bonnie said, "Doesn't it feel funny having the steering wheel on the right side instead of in the middle?"

"Yeah, well, it takes a little time to get used to it. But it really is fun driving this way."

Things were always wearing out on the farm. One day Jim said to Dad, "Dad, I need some new work shoes. These have holes in the bottom."

Bill said, "Let's see how things add up with your jobs. Besides Mr. Conners, you worked for Mrs. Blankinship making hay, Mr. Gordon making fence, and Mr. King walking corn and bean fields. You wear out your clothes earning money, then you should spend some of it to buy new ones."

From that day on, Jim bought all his shoes and clothes. It made him feel grown-up and responsible.

One afternoon, Bonnie, Frances, and Jim were riding home on the school bus. As they approached the farm, they could see big yellow machines in the barnyard. Jim asked, "What are those yellow things?"

Bonnie said, "Probably just some new toy Ray bought?"

A curious Jim was the first off the school bus. He ran to see the new things. He stopped short gaping at a huge Caterpillar, dirt scoop, and bulldozer blade. He was wide-eyed with awe. Bill, Uncle Young, and a man he didn't know were in a conversation.

Jim interrupted. "Where's the Allis Chalmers Caterpillars?"

Bill, casting him a stern look, said, "The boss sold them, and this is the replacement. Now please don't interrupt folks who are talking."

Uncle Young, shaking his head, was saying, "Boy, a D-8 Caterpillar! When I was up in Canada and Alaska working on the Alcan, we had little D-4 Cats. We weren't getting much done until we got the D-8s. Then progress really picked up."

Bill turned to Jim. "Jim, this is Tom. He's the operator."

Tom said, "Jim, your first lesson in Cat skinning. Only the Caterpillar Company makes Caterpillars. Everything else is a crawler. Stick with me, and you'll be a Cat skinner in no time."

Jim beamed at the idea.

It was late winter, and Tom was pushing manure out of the feed lots with the D-8. Sometime later, he drove the Cat up to the water tank and shut it down. Bill said, "Kinda early to quit for the day, isn't it?"

Tom was eagerly getting down. "It's Friday, payday, and I've got a date. Gotta get cleaned up and get back up to Avoca."

Bill cocked his head. "Aren't you even going to wash off the tracks?"

"It's warm. It'll be okay over the weekend. I'll wash it off Monday night." He was eager to go and couldn't be talked out of washing off the tracks.

Bill walked away shaking his head. That evening, a cold breeze swept the farm; it started getting cold. By Saturday, the temperature dropped to below freezing. Bill, standing beside the D-8, was shaking his head and looking at the trucks covered with manure.

On Sunday afternoon, Alice was in the kitchen when Bill approached all bundled up against the cold. "Still below freezing," he said. "Boy, it's a lot of work keeping livestock alive. I sure hope that this cold spell can't last much longer."

When Tom arrived for work Monday morning, he tried to start the D-8. Bill, watching, was veiling a grin. It started up all right, but when Tom tried to move the Cat, he found it was frozen to the ground. He tried to rock the Cat back and forth but almost killed the engine. He began cussing.

Bill said, "Was that hot date worth it?"

Tom, flustered and angry, said, "I can't just wait for warm weather to thaw it out. I've got to do something."

Bill, his grin almost visible now, said, "The only thing I know is to get the hog-scalding vat, put it on blocks, fill it with water, and build a fire under it."

When more men arrived for work, Bill began directing them to keep pouring boiling water on the tracks, fill the vat with more water from the tank, and wait for it to get hot. By late morning, Tom was still trying to move the Cat. Finally, he was able to rock the machine enough to get it to move ever so slightly. After more herculean efforts, it finally broke loose from the frozen mud.

Do you think that maybe that was Tom's emotional event?

Farm society was not all work. Country folk took a lot of pleasure from some simple entertainment like square dancing. It was the social networking of the day. Every Saturday night, all would gather at a different house for an evening of square dancing to the music of a piano and a fiddle. Everyone brought something to eat.

This evening during the dance, Bill was in conversation with some other man. "How does the boss make his money? This farm doesn't bring in that kind of cash."

One said, "His business is slot machines and jukeboxes. The slots are illegal. He covers western Iowa, eastern Nebraska, and northern Missouri as well as southern Minnesota."

Bill's jaw dropped. "Isn't he worried about the illegal slots? Afraid they will be found out?" Another man had the answer. "Hell, everybody knows about it. Every time a raid is planned, he gets a call, and one of his men runs out and removes the slots. The thing he has to worry about is organized crime. The Pendagas gang down in Missouri told him to get the machines out of their area, or they were coming after him."

Bill said, "That must have put a dent in his profits." "Hell, he's still taking five, six, or seven a week." An amazed Bill said, "Wow, seven hundred."

The man grinned. "No, seven thousand."

Bill, awed, said, "So this farm is just a hobby."

One day, Ray Alverson, the farm owner, drove into the farmyard. He quickly found Bill in the barn. After they talked awhile, Bill called Alice. She came out of the house and joined them. Ray said to her, "How would you like to have either a pinball machine or a jukebox in the house?"

Bill and Alice exchanged a knowing glance. They chorused, "Jukebox."

Ray asked, "What kind of music."

They didn't need to consult on that either. Bill said, "Square dance, waltzes, and polkas."

Now the house was built with the kitchen, dining room, and living room all in a line with big wide doors. In the city, they called such a house shotguns because you could shoot from the front door, and it would go out the back. The jukebox was placed in the dining room.

Their farmhouse became the social center for the area. On dance nights, the big furniture would be moved to the enclosed back porch.

Alice announced some new arrangements to the kids. "Dad and I talked it over. Jean and her high school friends get the house on Friday evenings. Dad and I and our friends have Saturday evenings. Bonnie and Frances get the house Sunday afternoons with their friends."

Jim complained, "What about us kids?"

Mom said, "You can play outside or in the barn if it's raining."

The Pope place became a lively square dancing place complete with jukebox music, which of course was much more varied than the piano and fiddle. Also, the piano was limited to only a few houses.

CHAPTER SEVEN

Bill and the kids were standing by the hog lot. "Okay, kids, there are a few more crippled and runt pigs for you." These were the pigs that would yield the least profit and could be discarded.

Of course, the children always made sure their pigs got extra rations. But they were always sad to see their pigs, now full-grown hogs, loaded onto a truck for the market. They were like their father that way. The pigs were like pets to them, and they raised them from piglets.

Bill arrived home from the market with the kids' share of the hog sales. He sat at the kitchen table, and the kids gathered around him, excited to see what they each had earned. Bill said, "I already cashed the check. So here is the four-way split."

As he handed out the money, he asked, "What are you kids going do with all that money?" Jean said, "Now that I'm earning money doing housework, I'll need some new clothes." Bonnie's choice was, "I'd like to go to Seattle and see Grandma."

Jim had his own idea. "I think I'll buy a car. I see lots of them for sale and cheap." Alice piped in, "Don't be silly, Jim. You'll do no such thing."

Laughing, Jim acquiesced. "I guess I'll have to buy some work and school clothes." Franny said, "I'm going to buy a bike."

"Wow," was the unanimous reaction. "A bike!"

The next Saturday, the family made the run into town with a new objective: buy Franny's bike. While they scattered as usual, Franny went to the hardware store to look at bikes. In a while, she was fixated on a gleaming, new red Columbia. Enthralled and without taking her eyes off the bike, she told Bonnie, "Go find Dad. Tell him I found the bike I want."

When Bill arrived at the hardware store, he told Jim. "Go find Mom so she can look at it too." Driving home, the bike was tied securely to the back of the old yellow 29 Chevy.

When they got home, some of the excitement wore off when they realized that there was too much snow on the ground to try out the bike. Dad came up with a solution. He suggested, "Why don't we learn to ride the bike in the house. There's a pretty long and straight path from the front door to the back."

This idea got immediate approval.

Everybody took turns riding Fran's bike. Jim found it harder than the tractor. He wobbled, yelling, "Help, I'm falling." Everybody ran to catch him. Not in time as Jim hit the floor, arms flailing. The bike had some damage too. It had hit the coal bucket and broke the front headlight.

Even today, Jim feels sorry for banging up Franny's new bike.

It was now summer, and Bill was having a talk with Jim one morning. "Tom's going to fill in the big ravine on the back section to give us more crop ground. He's also going to build a dam. Tom thinks you'll be able to help him, so that's your job for the next couple of weeks."

Jim found the work fun. Riding the D-8 with Tom, as he pushed the trees and stumps into the ravine. The big dirt scoop, fuel truck, and lowboy were set off to the side. Tom showed Jim how to start the auxiliary engine and operate the Cat. Jim learned quick and soon looked like a pro, downshifting and wheeling the big D-8 back and forth.

Soon the ravine was filled in and the dam completed.

Tom had some instructions for Jim. "Instead of loading the Cat on the lowboy, Jim, why don't you walk the Cat around the road back to the barnyard? Stay in the ditch as much as you can so you don't tear up the road."

"What about the dirt scoop?" "You'll be pulling that."

As Jim passed a farm where a boy Jim's age was playing with toys in the yard, the boy stopped, waived to Jim, and stood watching as Jim passed.

Jim thought to himself, who needs toys? I'm a Cat skinner.

Jean was out in the yard hanging clothes. She saw the Cat coming down the road. She gasped and ran to the house, shouting, "Look what's coming down the road."

Alice, Bonnie, and Frances followed Jean.

Alice called out, "It's Jim driving the Caterpillar." Her voice was ambivalent, half pride and half concern. "Why would Tom let him do that? He's only in the fifth grade."

Jim walked the Cat up the driveway and into the barnyard. To show his skill, he made a right turn to park it by the machine shed. He pushed down hard on the right pedal and pulled back on the right lever. The D-8 let out a loud squawk and made a sharp turn pushing up huge mounds of dirt and gravel.

Hearing the loud noise Bill dashed out of the barn. Seeing what had happened, he ran out and jumped up on the Cat, clutched it out, and brought it to a halt. He then pulled Jim off the seat and pointed at the mounds of dirt and gravel. "Is that how Tom taught you to turn a corner?"

Jim's head hung low. "No."

"Now you park the Cat and get a shovel and fill in those ruts!" "But, Dad, I can just lower the blade and back up."

Bill locked eyes with him. "That's true Jim, but that way wouldn't be much of a lesson to you, would it?"

"Boy, that mound of dirt and gravel is sure hard to shovel."

Do you think this is another of Jim's significant emotional events?

Jim Pope and the D-8 Caterpillar as described on pages 32 & 33 of my story Post Hole Digger. I was in the 5th grade at Macedonia, Iowa.

Alice had two cents to add about the situation. "Bill, you have a talk with Tom. Jim's only in the fifth grade. He's too young to be operating that monster."

With a snicker and a grin, Bill said, "No, Ma. I think Jim just became a very good Cat skinner."

Just then Tom pulled into the barnyard with the lowboy. He called out, "Jim, come on. We have to get the fuel truck." Tom and Jim got in Tom's pickup and headed down the lane.

Alice cocked her head. "Now how can Tom get both vehicles back here?"

Bill just grinned and went back to work in the machine shed. Alice went back in the house.

In a while, Jim came driving up in Tom's pickup. Alice saw him out the window and, mouth agape, went to find Bill. When she did, she exclaimed, "Bill, now you have to talk to Tom!"

Bill simply nodded and didn't try to hide his smile.

When Tom pulled in the with fuel truck, Alice waved to him and called, "Come here, Bill wants to talk to you."

When Tom alighted from the truck, he found himself before both parents. Alice glanced at Bill, but when he said nothing, she demanded, "Tell him. Go on."

Bill held his tongue for a moment, and shuffling his feet, he said, "Ya know, Tom, if Jim gets any better with that Cat, you won't be needed around here." Both men snickered. Fuming, Alice stomped off into the house, muttering to herself.

One day Ray, the owner, came by. His son, about the same age as Jim, was sitting in the car. Ray said, "Bill I bought fifty-two head of Minnesota heifers and five bulls. I want to see a pasture full of calves."

Wide-eyed, Bill said, "We'll have to fence something off to keep the bulls separate." Ray didn't seem to hear but rather said, "How long until we can breed them?"

"If they're small, it'll be a long time."

Just then Jim pulled into the yard with the M Farmall tractor and shut it down. Ray's son, Jerry, jumped out of the car and ran over to the tractor. Instead of using the drawbar to get up on it, he tried to climb up over the rear tire. His foot kept slipping down the rim. Then he stepped on the valve stem and broke it off. Fluid came gushing out as the tire went flat.

Frowning, Ray muttered, "Damn clumsy kid. "Get on in the car."

The owner then got into the habit of calling Bill frequently to see if the heifers were ready to breed. Eventually Bill got frustrated with the calls and told him, "Look, Ray, when they are ready, believe me, I'll tell you. But they're not ready yet."

Bill knew his boss had a way of getting his way, and one day when he found the bulls in the pasture with the heifers, angry, he called over one of the hands. The man raised his hand in defense and said, "Bill, don't blame me. I couldn't stop him. He owns the place. He opened the gate. I know they're still too small. But try telling him that!"

Bill reined in his anger and asked the man, "How many do you think we're gonna lose because of this?" The man shook his head. "I don't know. But I'd guess quite a few."

The answer was to be had at calving time. Seven dead heifers littered the farmyard. Four dead calves lay among them. Inside the barn, Bill and Jim were pulling on another calf from his moaning, bawling mother.

Bill went into the house and got on the phone with Ray. He simply said, "Ray, your heifers are calving." An excited Ray said, "I'm on my way down. I want to see this."

A while later, a glum Ray was looking at the barnyard full of dead heifers and calves. While Bill was miffed, he held it in. Ray was rather philosophical about it. "Well, that project didn't work out."

Now Bill couldn't hold it in. "A project? These were healthy living animals."

In the most blasé manner, Ray said, "So? Things just didn't work out. Call the meat wagon. You just have to cut your losses and move on." Wordlessly, Bill gazed at the man and then walked off. Ray got in his car and drove off. Losing animals, especially so senselessly, irritated the animal-loving Bill. He held it against Ray.

CHAPTER EIGHT

Electricity had finally come to the farm. Everyone was thrilled at the idea of no more lamp and lantern cleaning or any more smelly, smoky kerosene. All the neighbors were talking about all the new electric stoves, cream separators, and milking machines. Bill said, "I'm holding off buying that stuff until I find out how stable the electricity is."

But the next snowstorm blew in hard, toppling trees and buildings and electric poles. The power went off, and the family was back in the last century. The neighbors that went electric were calling, asking to bring their milk over to separate and to cook meals.

Alice, always the skeptic, moaned, "I knew this would happen." Alice and Bill scurried to get lamps and lanterns ready. It kept snowing harder, and the wind grew in intensity as the day went on.

Jim was sound asleep, huddled under his comforter, when he was awakened by his father's voice. "Jim, get up. All the doors are snowed shut. The snow's up to the roof. We'll have to go out through an upstairs window, over the porch roof, to get to the machine shed for shovels and scoop our way back to the back door."

Bill and Jim crawled out an upstairs window and scooped their way back to the house to get the back door open. Alice and the girls shuffled their feet in the drafty cold and waited at the back door to get outside to the outhouse.

On the school bus on the way home from school, Bonnie and Fran discussed farm chores. Bonnie said, "It's time we started milking the cows to help Dad with the chores." Dad readily agreed but had his doubt about their idea of the difficulty of the job. Bonnie and Fran found out too.

The next evening found them sitting on each side of the same cow, trying their hand at milking. Bonnie was hopeful. "It isn't so hard."

Frances said, "Yeah, but that tail hurts when it whacks you." Bill came in. "How's the milking going, girls?"

Bonnie said, "One cow kicked the bucket over. I don't think we lost too much milk."

Bonnie and Frances were outside swinging, and Jim was playing with his dogs as Alice exited the house. Alice stopped and turned to the door. "Jean, while Dad and I are in town at the bank, when you get finished messing with your hair, get the kitchen cleaned up and mop the floor!"

As soon as Bill and Alice were out of sight, Jean came outside shouting at Bonnie and Frances, "Get in the house and get busy cleaning the kitchen!"

Bonnie said, "Mom told you to!"

Jean said, "I'm in charge when Mom isn't around. Now you and Fran get in the house and get to work." Bonnie and Frances started running away with Jean chasing them.

Jim ran to the plank sidewalk leading to the outdoor toilet, turning them over and gathering up a handful of worms, and started chasing Jean.

Jean, afraid of worms, ran screaming toward the house with Jim right behind her. She ran upstairs to her bedroom and slammed the door. Jim fed the worms under the door, trapping Jean in the room.

"Now, Jean, what are you going to tell Mom when she comes home and you're in your room and your work isn't done?"

Jean said, "Please, please get the worms. I'll do the kitchen."

Jean being afraid of worms, Jim always had the upper hand with her. And the seasonal cycle went on. Come spring, Tom told Jim, "We have some custom-terrace work to do. It'll take more time to load the Cat, unload, and reload it after we're done and then unload it back here. I'll have you walk the Cat to the job, and I'll follow with the fuel truck. There's a couple of small bridges along the way. When you get to the first one, stop. I'll show you what to do."

Jim braked to a stop at the first bridge. Tom got out of the fuel truck and approached the Cat. "I don't trust these old bridges, so I want you to move up close to the bridge in the center of the road. Put the Cat in low gear and engine speed just above idle. Let the clutch out and jump off. Let it walk across. If the bridge holds up, run across and jump back on."

Jim related it at the dinner table. He said, "Guess what I learned today with the Cat."

Alice turned a deaf ear. "I don't want to hear it. You're too young to be driving that thing." Bill chuckled. "Tom told me about it."

Airplanes were often used to spray farm crops. Bill and Jim were standing in a pasture beside a cornfield. Each had a pitchfork and a bushel basket. Bill said, "Now to mark the aiming point for the airplane, we'll stand at the end of the same row, place the basket on the end of the pitchfork, and hold it above the corn. When the airplane flies over, duck down and lower the basket over your head. When he passes and the air clears, count over thirty rows. I'll be at the other end of the field doing the same thing."

Later a flatbed truck with a tank on it drove across the pasture toward them. The driver stopped and asked, "Is this level enough for him to land? We don't want him to hit a hole and flip the plane."

Bill said, "Looks okay to me, but I'll drive around it a little to make sure."

Jim was standing between the rows of corn at the end of the field, holding the pitchfork with a bushel basket on it above his head. The aircraft, engine roaring, approached. Jim ducked down and lowered the basket over his head. A stinking gray fog sprayed from the plane's tanks and settled slowly over the field.

Jim hurried, counting off thirty rows and got ready for the next pass. As the pilot leveled out for his approach, he wiggled his wings. After the pass, Jim headed for the truck. The aircraft circled and landed in the pasture. The truck driver drove over and filled his empty spray tanks. Dusk came, and another farm day was over.

One day in the farmyard, Ray was talking to Bill. "Bill, it's getting too expensive to buy tankage for the hogs. I'm toying with the idea of buying slaughter horses for you to kill."

Slack-jawed, Bill was speechless. Eventually he said, "No hurry, we have enough tankage to last six weeks."

When he told Alice about it that night, both realized that their stay on this farm might be limited.

About a month or so later, Ray stopped by and asked about the tankage. Bill said, "We still have enough for a week and a half. Won't you reconsider buying horses to replace the tankage?"

"No, it's just smart business. I have to save money. The feed bills are killing me!" "Are you sure you won't change your mind?"

Ray was now almost belligerent. "No."

"Well," Bill said, "I love horses too much. I can't kill them for tankage. I'm giving you notice. We'll be moved out in a week." He turned and walked off.

The family was settling into the new farm. The hired man's house was on the far side of a long open- area yard from Paul, the owner 's house.

On Bill's first morning on the job, Paul was talking to him. "Bill, you won't see much of me for a couple of days. After the chores are done, I'm going to a livestock sale at Greenfield. Take a couple of days to look over the farm."

A few days later, Paul reminded him, "Bill, I've got a lot of business to tend to. You know what has to be done. Let me know if you need anything."

Bill and Jim went about their work. Jim was driving the tractor, and Bill, in the wagon, was scooping oats into the hopper on the endgate seeder. Later, planting corn, Bill was driving the tractor, and Jim was on the corn planter. After that, it was weed control. They were slowly getting the farm into good shape. So much so that talking to a neighbor over the fence, the neighbor commented, "Paul's farm never looked so good."

"Well," Bill said, "he sure let the place go downhill."

The neighbor 's next comment was flattering. "Paul sure got lucky when he hired you. With you and Jim, he got two for the price of one."

"Well, it's a lot of work. But I'm pleased the way the farm is coming back."

The neighbor said, "Better get used to working it yourself. All Paul wants to is drive that old White truck all over the country."

That evening Bill was talking to Alice. "I talked to some neighbors. They told me all Paul wants to do is drive around the country in his stock truck and take his wife to the city shopping. If he can't find people to run the farm, I believe he'd sell it."

Alice's brows shot up. "Well, you hear me, Bill Pope. If he tries to sell it, don't you go thinking of buying it."

Bill didn't answer but reserved his thoughts.

In the morning, Alice said, "Dad, if you don't need Jim's help for a while, I need some things from town."

"We only have one tractor, and I need it. He'll have to walk. It's not much farther than when we lived up North."

"Okay, I'll call the grocery store."

"Do that, Mom, but don't overdo it. It's a long walk." He turned to Jim. "Jim, take that old army backpack."

It was just a routine matter for Jim. Sometimes he liked the solitude of walking. On the way back, he stopped to plunk rocks into the river.

When he got home, Mom was on the phone. He heard her say, "Okay, Roy. He'll be there." She hung up the phone. "Bonnie, go find Jim."

Bonnie said, "He's already here, Mom."

"Jim, Mr. King needs your help haying tomorrow for a couple of days." Jim's reputation as a hard-working boy was getting around the community.

Later, another neighbor, Mr. Climber, drove out to the field where Bill was working. Bill greeted Chuck Climber, laughing. "Hi, Chuck. That's very thoughtful of you to come to help."

Chuck said, "I wish I could laugh. I've been laid up for a while and got behind. Do you think Jim can handle a tractor doing the first corn cultivating?"

Bill said, "Sure he could. You have to go so darn slow the hardest part of that job is staying awake." Jim had been hunting, and now he returned home carrying his dad's single-shot .22 and four squirrels. From the porch, Bill queried, "Only four?" "I only had five bullets."

"Well, four out of five isn't so bad."

"Should have five for five. I hurried a shot and missed."

"Okay, young man, let's see how good a shot you are. Set small medicine bottles on the top board of the fence posts."

Jim loved the challenge. He fired deliberately and hit every one.

Grinning, he turned to his dad "Okay, Dad. Now it's your turn to see how good you are." He set more bottles on the post.

Smiling, Bill took his stance, muttering, "That target is too easy." He aimed awhile and fired. Jim was stunned. The bullet cut off the stem of a foxtail weed growing up beside the post.

Bill, laughing, said, "I told you the target you put was too easy. That weed was bothering me."

Next day, as usual, Jim and his sisters came pouring off the school bus. When they got in the house, Mom said, "Jim, your father has something to tell you."

Jim hurried out looking for his dad and found him in the barnyard. "Mom said you have something to tell me."

"Yeah, four of us men are going up North pheasant-hunting next Saturday. There's room for one more, and they agreed to let you go along. I'll borrow a .410 shotgun and get some shells. When we start hunting, I know you can outshoot all of them, so never take the first shot."

When the hunt was over, Jim had his limit of three birds, Bill had three, and the three other men had four birds between them. The man with a Browning 12-gauge automatic shotgun, shaking his head, said, "I got one bird, and the kid gets three with a .410!"

The second man said, "He sure outshot me, and did you notice he never took the first shot?" Jim said, "You were just too hurried to get a shot off."

The first man said, "If that doesn't beat all, I get a shooting lesson from a twelve-year-old."

CHAPTER NINE

There was a crisis at the school this winter day as the freezing rain and snow pelted the schoolhouse windows. Mr. Pilling, the bus driver, entered the principal's office. He declared, "The hills on my route are just too dangerous to take the bus out."

The principal argued, "The other drivers are running their route."

Pilling was adamant. "I drive a tank wagon and was on some of those roads earlier. It's just too dangerous. I'll take the kids to my house for the night or bring food here for them, but I refuse to take the bus out!"

The principal said, "I'm a backup driver. If you refuse, I'll drive your bus." Pilling said, "I've driven trucks all my life, and I know it's too dangerous."

The principal was waiting by Mr. Pilling's bus when school let out. Bonnie Pope said to the principal, "Where's Mr. Pilling?"

"He thinks the roads are too bad, so I'm taking your bus route."

Country roads usually have a slight crest in the middle to allow for drainage. On one of the more dangerous roads, it goes down a steep hill with a curve at the bottom with a large ravine on the right side. As the bus approached the curve, the principal applied the brakes to slow down. The bus went into a skid, off the road, and rolled over and over down the ravine coming to rest on its side. The small children were screaming. The older kids were yelling, "Hold on! Keep your heads down!"

The older kids got the rear emergency door open and helped everyone out and attended to them. The principal was standing at the front yelling, but no one paid him any attention.

Two high school boys ran up the hill to Peterson's farm. Mr. Peterson saw them coming, and he and Mrs. Peterson ran out to meet them. The boys were gasping, "The bus upset in the ravine. We need help." Mr. Peterson called, "Ma, call the operator and have her put out a line ring." Then Mr. Peterson and the boys headed back down the hill.

Back at the site, farmers and wives on tractors had already arrived. Everyone was taken up to the Peterson farmhouse.

At the farm, Mrs. Peterson was checking the children. She said, "There doesn't seem to be any major injures." Then the phone rang, and it was Mr. Pilling. Mrs. Peterson listened to him and then addressed everyone. "That was Art Pilling. He's heading this way with a bus and a couple of gravel trucks from the rock quarry." All the kids cheered excitedly.

Everyone watched the road as the two gravel trucks and a school bus pulled into the farmyard.

When he arrived, Art Pilling told the kids, "I'm taking everyone to the school." The two gravel trucks, with the school bus following, headed back to the school.

At the school, a large crowd had gathered. Inside the school, the faculty was waiting along with the townsfolk, ready to hand out blankets. Women were in the kitchen, scurrying to prepare something for the kids to eat.

As you would imagine, the principal was no longer a school bus driver.

Just a day in the winter life of rural Iowa.

Alice's Aunt Cora was diagnosed with osteoporosis, which had gotten to the point that she could no longer take care of herself.

Around the Pope family dinner table that night, Alice announced, "Aunt Cora is coming to live with us. Her doctor says she can no longer take care of herself."

The next day, Bill and Alice were helping Aunt Cora out of the car. She was bent over almost double and walking with the aid of a four-legged walker. She was lamenting, "I hope I won't be a big bother."

Alice, helping her into her room, was busy getting her settled. "It's never a bother to help a family member, Aunt Cora."

That spring, Paul told Bill, "I've got some business to do over at Orient. Those three horses haven't been ridden since last fall. They're pretty wild. You and Jim get them in the barn. And we'll start riding them."

Jim liked this task. It made him feel like he was doing the rough work of a cowboy of old, which, in fact, he was. Bill and Jim chased the horses through the timber and pastureland. All of a sudden, Bill dropped to the ground, rolled up in a ball, and came to a stop against a fence. Jim was screaming, "Dad! Dad!"

Bill stirred slightly. "I guess I just fainted."

Jim was holding his dad until his breathing returned to normal and he seemed to be regaining his strength.

Bill muttered, "I think I'm okay now. I have to go to the house and change clothes." Jim helped him to his feet and supported him as they walked to the house.

Alice, seeing them coming, ran, screaming out of the house, "What happened?"

Bill said softly, "We were chasing those damn horses, and I fainted." Alice said, "Let's get you to bed."

Bill, still anxious about the farm work and still in command, said, "Jim, you'll have to do the chores. Mom, tell Bonnie and Fran to help with the milking."

Bill had been keeping up a brave front for the kids but confided to Alice, "Mom, I don't feel well. Have Jim stay home from school to help Paul."

Paul, hearing of Bill's condition, came over to the house. In conference with Alice and Bill, he said, "We have to get you to a hospital."

After extensive testing at the hospital, Bill's doctor entered his room. He looked grave. "Bill, your EKG tells a very bad story. You had a severe heart attack. Your test results show you've had problems in the past."

Bill, looking sheepish, said, "I thought those were indigestion, doc."

The doctor said, "You need lots of rest and no heavy lifting. In fact, if you stay with farm work, it will kill you. You have to find lighter work."

Bill's return home was a somber affair. He looked tired and beaten down by his ordeal and his new employment problems. Soon Bill was back to work.

But the kids were more confident as they thundered into the kitchen home from school. Bonnie had a flyer in her hand, and at the dinner table, she handed it to Dad. "Here, Dad. I saw this posted on the bulletin board outside the superintendent's office at school."

Bill took the paper with little enthusiasm. The poster read, "Mr. Nelson, our janitor, is retiring at the end of the school year. If anyone is interested in taking his place, contact Joe Johnson, school board president."

Bill handed the note to Alice, who was hovering nearby, the strain of life clearly on her face. After reading the note, her eyes lit up. "Bill, this is a godsend. Do you think they would hire you?"

Bill, his voice low, said, "I don't know. It'd be a lot of work figuring out how all the systems work." Still enthusiastic, Alice said, "Why don't you have a talk with Mr. Nelson?"

A bit more alert, Bill said, "That would give me a little better understanding of the job." Within a few days, Bill was at the schoolhouse talking to Mr. Nelson.

Mr. Nelson said, "The school has a real problem. I wanted to retire last year, but they couldn't find a replacement."

Bill's eyes wandered around the boiler room at the three big boilers and the maze of piping. Whistling under his breath, he said, "I don't know if I could learn all this stuff."

Nelson sounded like a salesman when he said, "You can do it."

Bursting out laughing, Nelson said, "I'm not moving, so I'll be close by if you run into a problem."

On an inspection of the boiler room school, Bill pointed to a cot in the corner behind the boilers. "Is that your wife's idea of a doghouse?"

"No!" Mr. Nelson burst out laughing. "You see, on cold nights, the boilers need round-the-clock tending, so on those nights I sleep here."

"What kind of tending?"

"In the middle of the night, when the coal is burned down, you have to shovel some more coal into the boilers. The stoker boiler is automatic. I fill the hopper before I go to bed and it's okay until morning."

Bill sighed and shook his head. "I don't know which is harder milking cows or scooping coal at two in the morning."

Nelson broke the lull in conversation that followed. "Come on, let me show you the janitor's quarters." Bill followed him down the steps, under the gym, to the quarters. As they walked, Nelson said, "I know that if I recommend you, the school board will hire you. Now if you can support your family for a couple more moths, you could go ahead and move in here. You could work with me, learning the school until I leave."

Bill's doubts were reflected in his voice. "I can't farm any longer. I've got to find lighter work, but I'm not at all sure I can learn all this."

Over his shoulder, Nelson said, "In this town of two hundred thirty seven people, I don't know where you will find anything lighter than this job."

Bill had to admit, "You're right. I'll take the job if the school board will hire me."

As they arrived on the ground floor, Nelson said, "Why don't I call Joe Johnson? He's right up the street at his store. I'm sure he'll come if he has a chance to talk to you."

Later, Nelson, Bill, and Joe Johnson sat together on the lower bleachers in the gym. Johnson didn't look or sound as confident in Bill's prospects as Nelson did. He said, "Bill, there are some real concerns. You've always worked as a farmer. Here, lives are at stake. There is always the danger of a boiler blowing up, fire in the kitchen, gas lines rupturing, as well as all kinds of plumbing problems. The janitor is required to have full knowledge on how to handle all these emergencies."

Nelson stepped in. "Keep in mind, Joe, Bill has two daughters in high school and a son who will be in junior high, so he has their lives to be responsible for too. In a sense, Joe, Bill has a dog in the race too. In addition, he'll have the extra help of his kids. That's a lot of extra help when it comes to cleaning all those windows."

Johnson thought that over. Then he said, "Bill, I'm in favor of hiring you, but I have to have the approval from the full school board."

The six members of the school board were assembled for the meeting. Joe said, "I called this special meeting to vote on hiring Bill Pope for the janitor job."

The first member said, "It sounds like with hiring Bill, we're not only getting a janitor but a whole workforce. I vote for him."

The second member said, "We all know Bill Pope. He's honest and a hard worker. He won't steal us blind."

The third member added, "All of us here that are farmers have hired his son, Jim, in the past. He's just like his dad. What an asset he'd be."

Joe looked around the table. "Anybody else has anything to say before we vote on Bill?" A member cleared his throat like he had something to say but didn't speak.

Johnson said, "A raise of hands please." All hands went up.

Smiling, Joe Johnson said, "Let the record show that the vote was unanimous. We'll introduce Bill as our new janitor at our next regular monthly school board meeting."

The regular meeting was right around the corner. Johnson addressed the meeting. "The board has hired Bill Pope to replace our retiring janitor. Mr. Pope will also be a backup school bus driver."

It was quiet in the audience. Then Paul jumped to his feet. "I object. When Bill worked for me, he had a severe heart attack and couldn't work any longer. What if he has a heart attack when he's driving a school bus full of kids?"

Bill now rose to his feet. He glared at Paul. "Since I'm no longer working for a slave driver, the doctor says I've recovered."

Johnson raised his gavel. "Then the hiring of Bill Pope as janitor and backup school bus driver stands. Bill and his family will move into the janitor 's quarters. He will not be paid for the two months until Mr. Nelson's retirement. That will give our new janitor extra time to learn how the school operates."

On a walk-through of the school building and the machinery by Mr. Nelson he sounded like a tour guide. Bill and Alice followed him quietly. "Kindergarten through sixth grade use the playgrounds on the east side. On the west side where the baseball and football fields are, the seventh through twelfth grades use it at noon recess."

The tour moved on to the janitor 's quarters.

Alice, murmuring low said, "All the years without an indoor bathroom, and now we have them all over the building."

Bill added, "With showers and hot and cold running water."

The family was rather intense as they settled down in their new and strange new home. On the first night, a series of creaks and loud groans got everyone's attention, and they all peered about, wide-eyed. Laughing, Bill said, "It's just the school building saying good night to us."

Bonnie said, "What causes that?"

Bill patiently explained. "During the day, all the steel in the building heats up. At night, it cools down, and all the steel contracts. That makes the noises."

Frances said, "Whew, I thought we had ghosts. Will it always do this?" "It will until it gets closer to winter."

The family, as usual, began to adapt to their new surroundings. Jim, at the post office, was talking to two school friends. "What do you town kids do for fun? On the farm, there are lots of things to do."

One kid said, "We ride our bikes."

Another said, "We go out to the rock quarry and play on the machinery. The river runs right past it, so we always find things to do."

Still another kid said, "But the real fun comes on train day. The freight train comes up here every Tuesday and Thursday. It goes about four miles up to Carson, turns around, and comes back heading South. If you give the three-man train crew a cigar, they'll let you ride up and back."

Jim was curious. "How do you get cigars?"

Someone said, "On train day, the café will sell us cigars, or our dad will buy them for us."

Later, Jim got a firsthand view of this pastime. They were waiting on the platform, cigars in hand. When the train pulled in, the depot agent told them, "The train has to drop a carload of lumber at the lumberyard before it stops here. You can run over there and catch it if you want."

The three boys ran up to the train engine, waving the cigars. The conductor said, "I see you got the right tickets. Who wants to ride in the engine, and who wants to ride in the caboose?"

One kid climbed up onto the engine compartment. Jim and a friend climbed up into the caboose. As the train pulled out, Jim and his friend, sitting high up in the cupola window of the caboose, waved to the towns-people who had gathered to watch.

Jim's friend said, "When we get to the end of the line at Carson, we'll change and ride in the engine coming back."

But the workday came all too fast. Mr. Nelson was explaining the various systems and how they operated to Bill and Jim.

Jim slapped his forehead with the palms of his hand. "Boy! I'll never remember all that." Nelson grinned. "Then you better take some notes."

By the time they got to the boiler room, Jim had a notebook and pencil in hand. The first thing he did was draw an outline of the build-ing. Murmuring to himself, he said, "The gas comes from the street here to the meter, cutoff valve, into the building here. Then it goes to the school kitchen cutoff valve, then to the chemistry lab, then to home economics room cutoff valve and the janitor's quarters. Seems simple enough."

Nelson reviewed Jim's drawing and nodded his approval. "You'll find that the electrical system is harder to understand. But it's the most important."

Nelson motioned for them to follow him. "Let's go on up to the maintenance shed." There he began to point out the equipment. "This is our self-propelled lawn mower. Jim, I don't know if you're big enough to handle this."

Jim grinned. "It doesn't even come close to a D-8 Caterpillar."

Now it was Mr. Nelson's turn to grin. "I've heard some pretty tall tales about you. Maybe they weren't so tall after all."

The next day out in front of the school building, Nelson said, "Well, Bill, here are the keys to your new kingdom. You've got all summer to learn the rest of the job. If you have any questions, I'm only a phone call away, and I'll drop by to see how things are going from time to time. Make sure everything's ready for the Saturday social."

Looking at the windows, Bill said, "Looks like a lotta pain." Nelson said, "With your work crew, it won't take long."

The family was in the gym, cleaning up. While they worked, Bill said, "Here's the plan for the summer. Jim, you'll take care of the school grounds. Mom, me, and you girls will inspect all the rooms and make a list of everything that needs to be done. A week before school, all of us will wash the windows."

On Saturday night, people were beginning to fill the gym. The floor was full of square sets. Women in the home economics room were setting out refreshments on the pass-through window to the gym.

The school gym was used for square dancing by the townspeople, and come Saturday night, the gym was full of people waiting for the dancing to start. But this Saturday evening, the dance caller called in, advising he was going to be about an hour late. When Mrs. Knowles got up and announced that the caller would be late, a groan went up.

Back in the home economics room, the ladies were trying to figure out how to entertain the crowd for an hour. Someone suggested games. That idea fell flat. Then Mrs. Knowles said, "Hey, you know, I think Jim Pope knows some of the calls. Someone find him."

Jim was a little shy but admitted, "Yeah, I know some calls."

Mrs. Knowles let out a sigh of relief. "Great, then you call the dance until Mr. Beck the caller gets here."

Jim said, "Sure, I need some help getting the record player set up."

When Jim got up on the stage, everyone did a double take at the adolescent. Someone said, "He's gonna call?"

Others shook their heads.

Jim took the mic and soon had the dancing going. He called to the beat of the music.

> Ladies do and gents you know
> It's night by right by wrong you go. And you can't go
> to heaven
> While you carry on so
> And it's home little gal a do-si-do
> And it may be the last time I don't know
> And oh by gosh and oh by Joe.

Jim had them swinging to and fro in no time, and everyone was having such a good time they didn't notice when Mr. Beck arrived. Wide-eyed, he watched the party in full swing. Beck had to acknowledge Jim's good work and called to the crowd, "What a great job! Folks, let's give a big hand to Jim."

A rousing round of applause followed Jim off the stage. Sunday was spent cleaning up after the Saturday social.

Come Monday, it was back to the grind for the Pope family. Jim was in the boiler room at the drafting table, Bill at the workbench. Jim said, "Dad, these system drawings have never been updated. They don't match what we have now."

"We'll have to trace them out and get new prints made."

"Yeah, and there's been so many change to the electrical system and also circuit breakers not marked. I don't know what to do."

Bill stroked his jaw. "Let's see if Mr. Nelson can help. And in the meantime, we should advise the board of what we found."

Bill and Jim were at the next school board meeting. Bill, with big rolled-up sheets of paper, was addressing the meeting. "Jim and I traced out all the utility systems, and Jim made up these drawings. We need to get new prints made up."

The board members looked over the drawings and muttered to one another and seemed impressed.

A board member said, "We've been lax about keeping things up-dated. Mr. Nelson had it all in his head."

The second member said, "We'll send these drawings to the district office and get new prints made. Good attention to detail," he said to Bill and Jim.

By the start of the school year, Bill had things pretty well planned out. To the family assembled in the cafeteria, he said, "School starts in two weeks, and we need to follow a plan. Bonnie will be respon-sible for the K through fourth-grade rooms. Frances, you'll have the fifth- through eighth-grade rooms. Jim will have all the high school rooms. It will include all hallways and restrooms in your area. Mom and I will have the rest of the building. On the days I'm called on to drive a bus, you three will have to help your mom and cover for me. I'll give you the extra money I get from bus driving. When the teachers start reporting next week, you'll help them to get settled in their classrooms."

Alice added, "I'll also be working the kitchen. That will add a little to the budget." Alice was helping to serve in the cafeteria when Jim approached the serving line. Alice, through tight teeth, ordered, "Jim, come with me."

She led the way to the storeroom where she grabbed Jim's shirt and shook him hard. "Your teacher told me she caught you throwing a spitball!"

Jim simply cowered, offering no defense.

"Let that be the last time I hear any such thing, young man. You have to remember, our family is running this school, and any bad im-pression you make reflects on all of us. Understood?"

Jim meekly nods his head.

"You don't want me to tell Dad about this, I'm sure."

Jim just stood silent and did not move.

There were many issues to deal with that Bill and Alice had never even thought about. Like the time Jim, laden with mop, bucket, and cleaning supplies, carried an armful of women's hygiene boxes into the high school girls' and teachers' restroom.

Before entering, he yelled out, "Anybody in there?" A female voice answered, "I'll be out in a minute."

When a person emerged, it was a female teacher who gave Jim a less-than friendly look. This would result in a problem that the Popes never ever considered.

Bill was called into the superintendent's office. He said, "Bill, some of the female teachers don't approve of Jim cleaning their restroom. The ones the high school girls and women teachers use."

Bill had to cover a grin. "Jim's worked on a farm all his life and has three older sisters. He knows all about female hygiene."

"Nonetheless, they feel it's a woman's job." Bill sat, stroking his chin.

The superintendent then said, "Bill, I found in this job that it's best to just avoid problems when it comes to dealing with the opposite gender."

Bill said, "How about having Jim do that chore after all the women have left the building?" "Good idea, just as long as he doesn't do it before six p.m."

Then there was the adjustment to Ma's family menu. Jim complained, "Do we always have to eat the same stuff twice a day?"

Alice said, "Be thankful the school cooks are allowed to take home any food items that can't be saved." Bill added, "Thanks to your mom's job, our grocery bill has really dropped. My pay is only $212 a month, and with her pay, we live pretty good. Now that your sister Jean has graduated and married, that also helps the budget."

Jim's adolescent hormones weren't about to agree so easily. He was in no mood to be grateful. He said, "It also means more work for us all."

CHAPTER
TEN

There were problems unique to the school setting that the Popes had little experience with and so had to adapt, like shoveling snow from the school sidewalks at 5:00 a.m.

When Jim was in the study hall that afternoon, a messenger came in and gave Mrs. Travis a note. She read it and announced, "The weather is too bad to go out, so you will have your noon recess in the gym."

Then she called Jim to her. "Come with me out to the hall." Jim wondered, What have I done now?

"Jim, we need some way to entertain the students during noon recess."

Jim let out an inward sigh of relief and offered, "They can clean and dry-mop the gym floor."

Mrs. Travis rolled her eyes. "I think I have a better idea. I can play the piano, and you can call some square dance sets."

Jim thought about it. "That'll put some fun in it."

Soon Mrs. Travis was at the piano, and Jim was calling square dance sets. Everybody was having a great time at this recess.

Jim continued to serve his school in other ways too. He was in the study hall one day when a messenger handed Mrs. Summit a note. She approached a boy and pointed to the door then another and then Jim. In the hallways, Mrs. Summit told them, "The coach wants to talk to you down in the locker room."

When the boys faced the coach, he told them of his problem. "I don't have enough high school boys out for baseball to make a team. The school board has authorized me to use eighth graders. I've selected three to play on the high school baseball team." This was quite an honor for an eighth grader, and soon Jim was playing baseball. He felt certain that he could earn a letter in baseball like the older team members.

One day Jim stopped to read a note on the bulletin board. It read, "LETTER DAY, Friday." Jim was getting excited. He and the other two boys hurried to find the coach.

Jim eagerly asked, "Do we get to go to the high school assembly for letter day?"

Coach Welks didn't out-and-out deceive them, but his lowered eyes should have been the clue. He said, "Uhh … we don't know. We're still formulating the plan for it. I'll get back to you."

By Friday morning, Jim and the two other boys were primed and ready for their letter. One said, "Mr. Welk should know by now."

The other boy said, "Mrs. Summit should know."

When they finally reached Mrs. Summit, she had bad news. "The school board has decided that the eighth-grade boys will not be awarded a letter."

Jim's jaw dropped. "How can that be? I had a higher batting average than half the team."

Even though the baseball team had a winning season and Jim had one of the highest batting average, the young boys were denied a baseball letter. This left Jim bitter. There are limits to adolescent understanding.

The last day of school was joyous for the kids, and they didn't run out of the school building; they roared out in an almost-frenzied glee.

Bill and Alice were watching. Bill said, "Now the real work begins." Alice, casting a worried look at her husband, said, "Just don't overdo it."

When she asked Jim how he felt considering he would be in high school next year, Jim had a negative answer. "I just want school behind me."

The school was a different place during the off months. Jim kind of liked the solitude. One Sunday morning, he was standing inside the school front doors, looking out across the school yard, when he spotted a girl sitting on the merry-go-round in the school yard. He watched her intently.

Eventually he left the building and started toward her. When she saw him approach, she jumped off the merry-go-round.

Jim called, "That's okay, you can sit there." "I don't want to cause any trouble." "Trouble?"

"I'm supposed to be at church." "Where are you from?"

"I live down by Henderson. My folks don't approve of my smoking and my boyfriend. As punishment, they make me go to church."

Jim grinned. "Better hurry, or you'll be late." Flatly she said, "I'm not going."

"What will your folks say?"

"They won't know. Dad drops me off, and I meet him at the pool hall after church." Shaking a cigarette out of a pack, she offered, "Here, you want one?"

"No," was Jim's reply.

Lighting up, she murmured, "I hope nobody sees me."

"C'mon, we can hide in that circular hedge under those trees."

They walked to the far corner of the school yard and entered the hedge circle and sat down under the trees. She finished her cigarettes, and they lay on their backs. "It's so peaceful here. I wish I never had to go back home."

"Thing must be pretty bad."

She looked at him from under lowered lids. "Here, lie close to me. It makes me feel protected." Jim lay down beside her. "How old are you?" he asked.

"Seventeen." Gazing curiously at him, she asked, "Have you ever kissed a girl?" "Uhhh … uh, no."

She leaned into him. "Here, let me be the first."

The kiss was warm, wet, and passionate, tongues swimming back and forth. As their lips were still locked, she took his hand and placed it on her full breasts. She murmured, "Unbutton my blouse."

His fingers trembling, he fumbled with the buttons.

She then took his hand and placed it on her bare breasts, and he felt a stirring in his loins. He was unable to speak.

She said, "Have you ever seen a naked girl?" Still tongue-tied, Jim shook his head.

"Let me be the first," she murmured as she began to get out of her clothes. When she was naked, she took Jim's hand and rubbed it all over her body. His excitement was mounting till it was near bursting. And when she caressed his crotch, she giggled and said, "Now that's what is supposed to happen."

She unzipped his pants, and Jim shivered as her bare hand glided over him. They lay locked in a passionate embrace, entangled and gasping.

The peal of the church bell abruptly broke the mood, and she scrambled to get dressed. "I gotta go." As she was leaving, she called over her shoulder, "I'll see you next Sunday."

All week as Jim went about his chores, he played and replayed the episode over in his mind as he waited anxiously for Sunday.

Looking for his dad, Jim went into the boiler room. "Dad, are you down here?" A weak voice reached him from behind the boiler. "I'm here."

Jim found his dad on the cot and very pale. "Dad, what's wrong?" "All of a sudden, I just felt so weak."

"I'll go tell Mom."

Bill protested. "No, I'll be okay as soon as I rest a little." "Your color is bad."

"You go back to work. I just need to rest. I'll be up and around soon."

When Jim found his mom wiping down tables in the lunchroom, he told her, "Mom, you should go down to the boiler room and check on Dad. He's resting, and he doesn't look good."

Alice was quickly with Bill. "Dad, you come up and go to bed for a few days. Jim can sleep down here and keep the three boilers going."

If Jim thought he was busy helping his father, when the whole job was on him, he found out what busy was. The alarm wakened him at 2:00 a.m.; he hurried to shovel coal for the boilers. He thought about the girl and Sunday as he shoveled in the wee hours of the morning.

Sunday came, and Jim and the girl were again behind the hedges. They began a hungry-kissing session that quickly sent him into a rapture like he had never felt before. She grinned naughtily. "Ready for some more sex education?"

Two naked bodies engaged in heavy foreplay. She said "Not having sex is like getting this fantastic gift and never allowed to take it out of the box." Jim was too busy to answer.

Bill was back to work on the K through sixth-grade restroom. Alice came in. "Don't overdo it, Dad. We don't want you back in bed."

Two months later, the girl was waiting for Jim to show up. When he arrived, they kissed. Quickly they went into the prone position, their hands busy on their naked bodies. Jim murmured, "Sunday will always be my favorite day."

The girl sat up and, with a sad voice, said, "Jim, this will be our last time together. I won't be seeing you anymore."

Jim, almost breathless, said, "Are you moving?" "Sort of. I'm ... I'm pregnant!"

Jim couldn't speak. He tried, but only a kind of stutter came out.

"The boy my folks don't like is the father. I'm going to live with him and his folks."

Jim was almost embarrassed at his own relief, which he did not dare show.

She kept talking. "I wish you were the father. There aren't many nice boys in these small towns."

The sound of the church bell, which had become their signal to bring their time together to a close, had the saddening sound of something ending and something else was about to begin. The world would never be the same for young Jim.

A quick kiss and she was gone from his life.

He began the inevitable second-guessing. What if that was me? Me, a father at my age. My life would be over. How would I be able to support a baby?

CHAPTER
ELEVEN

It was a new school year, and Jim was in the ninth grade. The teacher was speaking to the class. "First order of business. I'll pass a sign-up sheet around. Anyone interested participating in any of the listed activities, put your name under the activity."

Next we will be electing a class president. You'll have a week to campaign. You will vote at the end of the week."

On nomination day, Ronnie stood and announced, "I nominate Jim Pope." Patty got to her feet. "I nominate Norma."

Gary said, "And I nominate Doug."

During the next week, everyone nominated was campaigning except Jim. He had no time or interest.

On Friday, the votes were counted, and the class sponsor announced, "The ninth-grade class president is Jim Pope. Jim, do you accept?" the teacher asked.

Jim rather solemnly said, "I accept." While he had no idea what the duties of the class president were, he kind of liked being so popular.

It was Halloween already, and things were being planned at the far end of the football field.

On this particular All Saints night, kids were getting rolls of snow fence from the lumberyard and closing off Main Street. Livestock was turned loose inside the enclosure. They nailed a two-by-four on each side of the outdoor toilets and carried them inside the enclosure. Dancing erupted inside the enclosure. It was a wild scene.

There were consequences as all involved were to find out. The next morning, the town marshal called for a school assembly and addressed the students. "Now everybody had a lot of fun last night. Now it's time to get the toilets back where they belong. The owners are waiting to identify theirs. Get the livestock back, and clean up Main Street."

A loud cheer went up and the cry of "Hooray! A school holiday!"

Back to the work of being a janitor, Jim was wandering the hallways, calling, "Dad. Dad, where are you?"

Jim checked the boiler room. No Dad.

Then he heard his mom calling. He went toward her voice.

He was shocked when he found her; the color had drained from Alice's face. Her voice was shaking. "Jim, Dad's down in the apartment in bed. He's very sick."

Jim rushed to his dad's bedside.

Bill said, "I think I'll be here for a spell. It's up to you to keep the school running. I know you can do it. It's getting cold, so the boilers have to be tended at night."

After a weary night of shoveling coal at odd hours, Jim stumbled out of bed at 5:00 a.m., muttering, "Another great day."

Unlike other students, when Jim saw a messenger arrive at whatever class he was in, he tensed, knowing it could be trouble. And this messenger brought more trouble: overflowing toilets in the girls' restrooms. Unlike other students, Jim had to find time between classes to go down to the boiler room and check things out. Another time, a messenger brought the news that the shower in the boys' shower room wouldn't turn off.

But Bill eventually got a little better. At the supper table, Alice commented, "It's good to see you strong enough to join us at the table, Dad."

"Yeah. I think I'll be able to get back to work tomorrow." Alice softly said, "Just take it very easy."

The next day, Bill was pushing a broom in the hallway when Jim came up to him. "How's it going, Dad?"

Bill said, "I can't do much more than push this broom, I'm afraid." "That's help enough. We're able to take care of the rest of it."

The thanks at Thanksgiving was given by Jim as the family sat around the dinner table. "Let's give the Lord thanks that Dad is up and around again." This got a big smile all around the table.

About a week before Christmas, Alice told the kids, "Christmas is coming, but things will be a little sparse this Christmas. We haven't been able to do any shopping."

That evening while decorating the tree, Alice said, "Donia's Dye Mercantile doesn't have much of a selection. We'll wait until things improve around here."

On Christmas morning, Dad was late returning from the boiler room. Jim took off to look for him. When Bill didn't answer several calls, Jim got worried. Finally he heard Dad's weak voice. "Here I am." Jim followed the voice to the cot behind the boilers. "Dad, what's wrong!"

Bill weakly muttered, "Jim, I don't have the strength to get up. Help me to the bathroom." Supporting Dad, Jim entered the apartment. Alice screamed, "Dad!"

Bill said, "No. It's okay, it's Christmas Day. I want to be here with the family."

But a solemn mood gripped the family. Alice firmly said, "Your working days are over for a while. Maybe until the end of the school year."

Jim got a call on Christmas Day. It was Harold Hodder calling to ask for Jim's help at his barroom that afternoon. Harold said, "I could use your help, Jim, but not if it's going to spoil your Christmas."

Jim said, "That's okay, we'll celebrate later today."

As they worked around the bar together, airing out the bar and cleaning up, Harold asked, "Was Santa good to you?"

Jim couldn't hide his frown. "Things are pretty sad. Dad took a turn for the worse, and he's bedridden for a while."

"I'm sorry to hear that, Jim. The whole town is concerned about your dad."

Back at the boiler room, Jim hung the new 1953 calendar and circled March 25.

Watching, Alice said, "You'll be sixteen this year. Won't be too long, and you'll be on your own out in the world."

"I can't wait."

Aunt Cora's care, along with Dad's illness, required more work from the family. Fixing Cora's dinner, Alice called, "Bonnie, take this tray to your Aunt Cora. And Jim, take this tray to Dad." It was sad to see both Aunt Cora, who used to be full of fun, and Dad, who was always so busy, now confined mostly to their beds.

Now it was up to Jim to shoulder the full responsibility of running the school.

"No, I just wish this winter would go away. I wish getting up every night at 2:00 a.m. to tend the boilers would go away."

A week before his birthday, Jim drew an X through the seventeenth.

Alice, watching, said, "One more week, and you'll be sixteen. It'll be a sad birthday with Dad sick in bed."

Jim said, "I'm going in right now to see how he is before I finish the day's work." At his bedside, Bill asked, "Are you taking good care of the school?"

"The school's okay, but my schoolwork isn't."

Turning sad, Bill said, "I know it's tough for you, getting called out of class to fix problems." "If I don't have everything done by ten, I quit and finish up in the morning."

"Are you able to sleep with all the noise?"

Jim grinned. "I'm so used to it I hardly notice it. The only time is when the tones change because of a problem. That wakes me up."

"Well," Bill said, "the worst of the winter will be over in two or three weeks." "Thank goodness."

"Yeah, but as you know, now with Frances having graduated and off to work in Omaha, our workforce is getting smaller."

Jim was asleep in the boiler room when his mother's scram from the top of the stairs jarred him awake. "Dad's had a heart attack, come quick." Jim glanced at the clock. It was 4:17 a.m. "Jim! Jim!"

Jim jumped up and ran up to the apartment.

Jim dashed to his father's bedside, where he found Bonnie, Mary and Mom sobbing hysterically. Bill seemed to be unconscious.

Jim asked, "Have you called the doctor?"

Mom said, "Yes, but he's twenty-five miles away. He is on his way. I hope he gets here soon."

When the doctor came in, he asked no questions but went to Bill and managed to get a pill in his mouth. Bill was groaning, semiconscious. The doctor motioned for everyone to leave the room.

Later in the apartment kitchen, the doctor explained to them. "It was a massive heart attack. He's resting, but keep checking on him." Placing a bottle of pills on the kitchen table, the doctor said, "If he has another occurrence, place one tablet under his tongue." On his way out, he said, "There's nothing more I can do for him. I'll check back later this morning."

After the doctor left, Jim rushed about his duties to get the school building opened up. Alice said, "I'll stay with him until I have to leave for the school kitchen."

Jim nodded. "I'll check on him after the first period." Bonnie added, "I'll see him after the second period."

In his classroom, Jim kept checking the clock, unable to concentrate on his studies. When the bell rang, Jim dashed down to the apartment to check on his dad.

Jim said, "You must be feeling a lot better. You sure had us scared." "Just another minor setback."

"That's not what the doctor said."

"He's just trying to drum up more business."

"Well, Bonnie will be down after next period."

Bill said, "No need for that. I'm feeling much better." As he finished speaking, a violent convulsion shook him, and he clutched his chest. Jim grabbed for the pills. Sitting on the edge of the bed, holding his dad, he tried to get the pill under his tongue. But Bill's jaws were clenched tight in agony.

Suddenly the man's body went limp.

Jim, rocking his father in his arms, cried, "Dad! Dad! Don't go!" Gently, the boy lowered his father down on the bed.

Still panicked and unable to face the truth, Jim dashed across the gym, down the hallway to the school kitchen. He found his mother there. Almost unable to speak between his gasping and sobbing, Jim blurted, "Mom, Dad … Dad … Dad died!"

Bill Pope was buried in the family plot in Avoca, twenty-five miles away.

The family was numb with grief. When they got back to the school, they were surprised to see Mr. Nelson and the faculty hard at work, cleaning and running the school.

Jim, alone, went to the relative quiet of the boiler room, sat on the cot, and sobbed. However, there was no time for grieving as it was winter and there was a lot of work to get done.

A couple of days later, Frances and Alice sought out Mr. Johnson in his hardware store. He greeted, "Hi, Alice. Hi, Fran . Don't tell me you're going to buy a TV?"

Alice intoned, "This is much more serious."

Joe could not hide behind his humor, so he said, "I know it's a terrible time for you."

Alice got right to the point. "Would you be able to let us stay as janitors until the end of the school year?"

Joe thought it over. "That's something the school board has to decide. I'll call a special closed-door meeting."

That evening, the board met in the lunchroom. Joe addressed the board. "I've been approached by Alice concerning letting them stay on as janitors until the end of the school year."

A palpable silence filled the room.

Eventually, a member broke the silence, "I haven't heard any complaints about their work." Another member added, "Jim has sure done a good job filling in while his dad was up and down." Another member said, "I'm amazed at Jim's boiler knowledge. I say not only keep them until school lets out. How about permanent?"

Joe panned the members around the table. "Anybody else got anything to say?" He again surveyed the members. "Well, then, we'll vote. Should it be a secret vote?"

A member said, "No. Voice vote. Right now." Joe said, "Any objections?"

Joe said, "All in favor of keeping the Pope family as janitors until the end of the school year, say yea." After another silence, they voted. All votes were positive.

Joe said, "The motion carries."

Back at the apartment, Alice was talking while fixing Aunt Cora's supper. "We're okay till the end of the school year. After that, I don't know what we'll do."

Bonnie said, "How about just staying here?" Jim was adamant. "No!"

A few days later, Mary advised them all to go into Aunt Cora's room. Once in the room, everybody sang Happy Birthday to Jim.

Happy sixteenth birthday. To this day, I miss my father, and as each birthday approaches, I feel the sadness.

After the festivities of the birthday song, Alice lapsed into seriousness. She said, "I don't know what to do. July will be here soon, and we have to move."

Aunt Cora broke a prolonged silence. "I could tell my renters they'll have to move, and we can move back to Avoca."

Jim and his mother exchanged a knowing glance. Alice was getting interested. She said, "It's a lot bigger town. Employment should be easier to find."

At the first school board meeting after Jim became the full-time janitor, Jim gave the state-of-the-school report, "The gym floor can't be refinished due to the nails showing."

Silence as the board members considered options.

Mr. Johnson said, "We don't have much extra money in the budget."

A board member said, "If we have another bad winter, the extra cost will break the budget." Jim injected, "The best I can do is use a nail set and drive the nails a little deeper."

Mr. Johnson said, "The Iowa State Board of Education report states that a school must have a minimum of 150 students K through 12 to sustain itself. We only have 125 students. It's only a matter of time before we'll have to merge with other schools."

A pause to consider the options.

Mr. Johnson said, "Let's vote. Vote yes to refinish the gym floor, or vote no and have Jim set the nails deeper."

A unanimous no vote carried.

As the family thought things over, Jim wandered by the school bulletin board. A notice said LETTER DAY Friday.

Jim couldn't participate in sports due to his dad's health. The ninth grade boys that played sports were not given letters.

Jim thinking "I'm done with this goddamn school!"

The school year ended, and with a combination of exuberance and melancholy, the kids poured out of the building.

During dinner that night, Alice asked, "How long will it take to close the school?"

Jim said, "About a month and a half. I need to get the boilers ready for inspection. That's the hardest part."

Jim got busy on that task. He was covered with soot when he finished brushing out the flues and tube and cleaning out the fireboxes and preserving the flue tubes.

When Jim contacted the Iowa State boiler 's inspector 's office, he was told he would be inspected in about a week or a week and a half.

Jim was working out front of the school building, when a car drove up and a man got out. Jim stopped his work and asked, "Can I help you?"

The man flashed a badge with large letters F B I.

Jim looked stunned F B I, what have done? Jim's mind was racing, trying to figure what he'd done wrong.

The man broke into a big grin and said, "Read the small print. It read Full Blooded Indian."

Laughing now, the man said, "I'm the Iowa State boiler inspector. I'm looking for a Mr. James Pope." Jim said, "That's me!"

The inspector cocked his head. "How old are you?" "I'm sixteen."

"And you're the janitor of a consolidated school?" "Yep." Jim grinned. "This is my kingdom."

The inspector said, "Okay then. Let's get this bloodbath, I mean, boiler inspection started." A puzzled Jim said, "Bloodbath?"

The man shook his head as if bewildered. "So far, every boiler I've inspected has failed, and I have to go back two or three times before they pass."

Jim escorted the inspector to the boiler room. When the man saw the cot, he said, "Is this where you hide out?"

Rolling his eyes, Jim said, "When it gets real cold, the hand-fed heating and hot-water boilers have to be tended to in the middle of the night."

"And you sleep down here?"

Jim picked up his alarm clock and showed the inspector. "It's set for 2:00 a.m."

The inspector checked the paperwork. "I can't believe it. This school hasn't had one discrepancy or problem in three years."

Jim, beaming with pride said, "That's when our family took over as janitors."

The inspector looked at his paperwork and read, "Bill Pope, janitor, died March 18, 1953." Then he dropped his head, shaking it back and forth. "Are you okay?"

The man said, "No. just some disturbing findings at one of my other inspections."

The man then, flashlight in hand, went about peering into the boilers interior while Jim explained the operating procedures for the three boilers and the safety features.

The inspector, clipboard in hand, began checking off blocks on his form. Then he handed Jim the certification.

With a smile, he said, "I'll leave you to your kingdom." He started up the stairs, stopped, turned, and looked at Jim. "How in the hell does a fifteen-year-old kid learn all this stuff?"

Then he continued up the stairs, muttering, "Boy, have I got a story to tell."

Jim tacked the certification on the bulletin board, gathered his belongings, and started up the stairs. At the top, he turned for one last look.

CHAPTER
TWELVE

A family friend drove us back to Avoca. A livestock truck came to a stop in front of the house. The sign on the truck read Schueman Trucking, Avoca, Iowa. Two men were unloading furniture as the car pulled up. Alice helped Cora out of the car. Aunt Cora, severely bent, was helped into her house.

Alice asked, "How does it feel to be back in your own house, Cora?" "Brings back so many memories. Both good and bad. When Ed's health got so bad that we had to close the icehouse, things really went downhill fast."

Alice said, "I bet some of your old friends will come by to see you." Cora's eyes were wistful. "I hope so."

The next day, Alice was walking through the two-block main street of the town of Avoca, stopping at each store, looking for work. When she found a Help Wanted sign at the Chatterbox Restaurant, she went in and asked for the manager.

When he came out in front he and Alice immediately recognized each other. The manager said, "Alice, I didn't know it was you. I'm so sorry about Bill." "Yeah, thanks. It's been rough. I'm just now able to function."

The manager said, "I know you were a cook at the Donia School. That's good enough for me. Start as soon as you can. On the nights when there are school activities, you'll have to work until closing time."

Jim too was looking for work. "Mom, I've got to find summer work."

Alice said, "What can you do? All you really know is farming." Jim thought for a moment. "I'll put up notices all over town."

Alice said, "I've got a better idea. Why don't you go up to the Journal Herald office and put an ad in the paper."

A while later, Jim was in the Avoca Journal Herald office. A female clerk asked, "Can I help you?" "I'd like to put an ad in the paper." "What kind of ad?"

"I'm trying to find a job of some kind." "What do you want the ad to say?"

Jim said, "Farm work wanted. Need help plowing corn, making hay? Call Jim Pope."

The clerk enhanced the ad. She said, "Let's say, need help cultivating corn? Making hay? General farm work? Does that sound better?"

"Yeah, it does."

"The paper comes out once a week. How many times do you want it to run?" "How much does it cost?" "Twenty-five cents a week."

"Okay. Run it two weeks."

Several days later, the phone rings in a rural Neola town farmhouse. A woman working in the kitchen answered.

The voice on the phone said, "Vonda, have John call right away." "He's in the field."

"Have him call me when he comes in for lunch."

Later, a man driving an Oliver 88 tractor drove into the farmyard, got off, and went into the kitchen. Vonda Koch was working at the wood-fired cook stove. "John, your sister, Alice, called, wants you to call her back."

"Hi Alice. What's up?"

"The Pope boy that was the janitor of the Donia schoolhouse has moved back to Avoca and has put an ad in the paper, looking for summer farm work. Thought you might be interested?"

John said, "You bet I am. He's young, but he's got a big reputation. I'll call him."

"I know the family farmed in Avoca and down at Macedonia. They were janitors at the schoolhouse when Bill died."

John said, "That happened not too long ago. Give me the phone number. I know some Macedonia farmers . I'll talk to them."

That evening the phone rang at the Pope house. Alice answered. "Hello, Pope residence."

John said, "Hi, I'm John Koch. I farm over by Neola. I'm looking for a hired man. Is Jim there?" "He's out on the porch. I'll get him."

When Jim got on the phone, John introduced himself and asked, "Tell me what kind of farm work have you done?"

Jim said, "We had nine tractors and D-8 Cat. I drove all of them and used all the machinery. Farmalls, Ford, John Deere, Massey Harris, Case, Oliver."

John said, "I have an H Farmall and an Oliver 88."

"The Oliver 70 Row Crop was my favorite. Having only one front wheel, if the tire goes flat, you're stuck."

John said, "What kind of machinery have you used?" Jim said, "Just about anything to do with tractors."

John was thinking to himself, Sounds like a loudmouthed kid trying impress me. John said, "Maybe I should ask you, what machinery haven't you used?"

Jim said seriously, "I've never run a hay baler, but I've sat on both sides of a hand tie, poking, blocking, and tying."

"What was the dangerous part of the job?"

"Making sure you kept your feet on the footrests. If you let them dangle and you crossed a ditch or a baler wheel falls in a hole, your legs get broken. I haven't operated a corn picker or a corn chopper either."

John thought for a moment. "How about I come to Avoca Sunday afternoon, and we can talk some more? By the way, how old are you?"

Jim said, "I'm sixteen."

That Sunday afternoon, a pickup braked to a halt in front of the house. Jim went to greet the man.

John said, "Hi, I'm John Koch." As John came inside, Jim asked, "What else do you need to know?"

"Nothing, I guess. I'll be honest with you. I thought you were some punk kid trying to impress me. I talked to some folks down at Donia. So you lived on the hobby farm. Everyone knows about it. James Conoyer told me he watched you operate a D-8 Caterpillar."

Jim paused then said, "With nine tractors, you had to stop and re-member which one you were on, where everything was."

John said, "Okay, I'll hire you for a one-month trial period. The pay is $125 per month, room, and board."

"When do you want me to start?"

"Right now, pack some clothes. We need to get back for chores."

On the front porch, Jim with an old ragged suitcases in hand, said good-bye to his mom and little sister, Mary. Mary was weeping.

Jim smiled and patted her on the head, and then John and Jim got in the pickup and drove off.

I've always felt sorry for my sister Mary. Nine years old at the time and had to be left alone while mom was working. Sometimes mom didn't get one until after 11:00 pm.

During the ride to Neola, John asked, "Have you ever had any work where you stayed overnight?" "Yeah. I had one job walking corn and bean that lasted three days. It was too far away to go home at night."

John grinned. "I hope you don't get too homesick."

Jim asked, "Homesick for what? Sleeping in a boiler room?"

"I know. I talked to some people down at Donia. I can't believe all that happened in your life. Sorry about your dad. He must have been a wonderful man."

Jim dropped his head and was quiet. John reached over and put his hand on Jim's shoulder. Changing the subject, John asked, "Do you still remember how to milk?"

Grinning now, Jim said, "That's something you never forget. When I stayed at the job overnight, I always helped with the chores." "I hope they paid you extra."

"Some of them didn't think a boy needed to be paid very much. How big is your farm?"

"I have three hundred and seventeen acres. But I rent two other farms and feed quite a few head of cattle."

"How big is your family?" "My wife, Vonda, and my two-year-old daughter, Sheila." Jim asked, "How many milk cows do you have?"

"Five." Looking at the sun, he said, "We should get home about chore time."

At the farm, Jim was curious about the machinery. "Where do you keep the rest of the machinery?"

John grinned. "The hobby farm got you spoiled. I have all the machinery I need to run the three farms. Do I want more? Sure. Do I need more? No. Unlike that fantasy farm, this farm has to make a profit. You have to have enough money in reserve to last three years in case of crop failures."

Not realizing it at the time, but that statement became the basics for my plan for life. When I got a piece of steel in my eye and I had to pay the doctor's bill, my father dying at such a young age, I interpreted that to mean find a job with medical benefits, a good savings, and retirement plan. A lot to consider at age sixteen.

John and Jim entered the farmhouse kitchen. John introduced his new hand to his wife, who was working in the kitchen. "Vonda, this is Jim. He said he'll give the job a month's tryout."

Jim just nodded to the woman. "Ma'am."

Vonda said, "What a polite young man. Sheila is asleep, so you can meet her later. But for now, I'll show you to your room."

Jim followed her into the bedroom. It had a window on two sides, making it bright and airy. Vonda turned back the covers, saying, "John's sister told me all about you. I hope this is better than a cot in a boiler room."

Still a bit reserved, Jim said, "It's a great room."

When she left, Jim began putting his things away. The sound of cows balling got his attention, and he hurried to change into his work clothes.

When Jim got down to the kitchen, Vonda told him John was getting started. Jim said, "I guess I better too."

As Jim walked across the barnyard, he paused to look at two huge lots full of fat cattle. When he got to the barn, John had all five milk cows lined up feeding.

John said, "If we don't do the milking, you don't get paid."

Jim cocked his head. "What does my pay have to do with milking?"

"Well, I look at it this way. Your salary is a hundred and twenty-five a month. We make about that much selling cream."

Jim smiled. "I better get busy pulling tits."

John approached a cow with shackles in hand. "This one you have to put shackles on." Jim nodded, and the two got busy. He asked, "How many head of fat cattle do you have?"

"Five hundred head on full feed. I've got another three hundred head of feeder cattle on the farm I rent from a church in Minden. I don't have any livestock on the Stageman's farm that I rent."

Jim asked, "Five hundred head? How many trucks will it take to get them to the Omaha stockyards?" "One or two."

Jim looked puzzled. "How can you haul five hundred head with only two trucks?"

John said, "I learned a long time ago that I can't outguess the market. Every time I have a load or two ready, I send them. If you continuously send cattle to market, you'll hit the market average."

Little did Jim know the impact of that conversation would have on him in later life. I think it was in 1980, and the new investing tool was called dollar cost averaging. The broker explained how you could invest a little each month and always be guaranteed hitting the market average. I laughed at him, telling him to go back to his college and demand his money back, that he was taught thirty-year-old information. I told him if he had known John Koch in the mid 1950s, he would have known all about hitting the market average. I told him that I had a PhD, and it was a post-hole digger. I stopped getting calls from brokers.

Jim still had more questions. "How many acres do you farm?" "It's right at one thousand."

Jim looked around. "I can see why you need help."

John frowned. "Well, I have hired help in the past, but it never worked out." "What was the reason? I'll try not to make the same mistakes."

John grinned. "They didn't work out because they didn't work."
Later, Jim was in the basement, turning the hand separator.

Watching him work, John said, "I'm thinking I got a bargain when
I hired you."

Jim kept working. As soon as he finished, John said, "I'll slop the
hogs. You take the cream can and set it in the water tank." The two
seemed to be getting a good teamwork going.

Later in the kitchen, Vonda and Jim were cleaning the separator
parts when John came in. "I went down to the basement to bring up the
parts for washing, and guess what?"

Vonda said, "Jim already brought them up. I washed and dried. He
even put all the disks back together." Jim said, "I'll take them back down
and put the separator back together."

When John reached over to help, Vonda held his hand and shook
her head. John nodded. Jim left with the separator parts.

Vonda said, "We'll know in the morning if he did it right." John
said, "I bet he will."

Vonda, veiling a grin, said, "What's the bet?"

John, looking smug said, "We'll settle that in bed tomorrow night."

Vonda, now unveiling her grin said, "Now I really like our new
hired man."

At the supper table the next night, Vonda asked Jim, "Is there any
food you don't like?" "No, ma'am, I eat anything that's put on the table."

Vonda looked at him. "That's unusual to hear a boy say that."

Jim told them the story of the two pig turds. "My folks made sure
we weren't picky eaters." Vonda said, "Good. You can empty all the
dishes on the table, but I won't cook anymore." When John and Jim were
working, Jim asked, "The two horses. Do you use them?"

"They're the last team I had when I farmed with horses. I keep them
for sentimental reasons."

Jim looked pleased. "Can I ride them?" "Sure, just don't do any
running."

"You still have the harnesses?"

John said, "Yep. It's all hanging in the machine shed. There's beer in the fridge. Anybody that does a hard day's work deserves a beer. You don't have to ask, just get one."

In the farmyard, John and Jim were standing by the H Farmall. John said, "We'll put the cultivator on the H, and you can get started with the first corn cultivating. First thing is to mount it."

Jim said, "We'll need to put a shield on for the first time through."

John smiled in approval. "Boy, you do know something about farming."

Several days later, in the farmyard, John said, "I've got a couple of days of custom-baling to do. Take the pickup, and drive over to the church farm, and check on the feeder cattle. Then take the H down to the Stageman farm, and start the second cultivating."

As John went to the 88 Oliver to hook up the New Holland baler, Jim got in the GMC pickup.

At the church farm, Jim checked the water in the creek and the amounts of grass. Then he looked over the young cattle. After that, he went back and got on the H Farmall to start cultivating corn.

Late that afternoon, Jim drove the tractor back into the farmyard. Vonda went out to meet him. She said, "I'm going down to get John. He's leaving the tractor and baler there until he's done." With her little girl in tow, Vonda got in the pickup and drove off.

Jim was in the basement, separating milk, when John came in. He asked, "All done with the milking?" Laughing, Jim said, "Gotta get this cream so I can get paid."

Shaking his head, John said, "I know I hit the jackpot when I hired you." Jim wasn't the needy type, but he appreciated his boss's approval.

John then picked up two buckets and said, "I'll slop the hogs."

When supper was over that night, as they sat at the table, John said, "Jim, would you consider working here for the rest of the summer?"

Joking, Jim paused, feigning deep thought. "I guess I can put all my other obligations on hold."

John said, "Okay, then it's settled. We'll take turns doing weekend chores. You'll have every other weekend off, and I'll need you on the weekends during the school year."

Sheila interrupted him. "Will you push me on the swing, Jim?" Vonda said, "It's almost bedtime for you, and Jim's tired."

Jim intervened. "I always have time to play with her." Vonda said, "Okay." Sheila followed Jim out the door.

CHAPTER
THIRTEEN

Jim was scooping feed into the self-feeder in one of the fat cattle lots when John approached. "Did you cash the paycheck I gave you? Vonda can't balance the books."

Thinking, Jim said, "No, it's still on my dresser. I keep forgetting to take it with me."

"Okay, when we go in for lunch, give it to Vonda. She's given you a new check for two months' pay." Days later, John came home to find Vonda beside the house on a stepladder with a long handle brush and a bucket of soapy water. She was scrubbing a yellow streak off the side of the house.

John gazing with a puzzled expression, said, "Why are you washing the house?" A disgruntled Vonda blurted, "See that yellow streak?"

John stared for a moment and then said, "Oh boy. That's gotta change."

Vonda intoned, "Instead of coming downstairs and going to the outdoor toilet, he's been peeing out the window."

John shaking his head, said, "Something's got to be said to him."

The next morning at the breakfast table, John asked innocently, "Vonda, what did your aunt and uncle do about their hired man that kept peeing out the window?"

Jim went stiff. His eyes lowered. The food on his plate mentally turned to rocks.

Vonda said, "Well, the cure was to make him wash the outside of the house every Sunday. He finally decided he could do better elsewhere and quit."

John scratched his head, perplexed. "Good help is hard to find. I'd sure hate to lose a hard-working hired man."

The rest of the meal was finished in silence.

For Jim, that was a value system changing, a significant emotional event. Many, many years later, I was attending a management seminar. The facilitator made a bold statement that the only way a person changes his value system is through a significant emotional event. It struck me funny, and I made a muffled sound.

The facilitator said, "Mr. Pope, I don't see anything funny about that statement. Would like to share?"

I said, "Hell, I learned that lesson when I was sixteen years old, one morning at the breakfast when I was told I shouldn't pee out the upstairs window because it leaves a yellow streak down the side of the house."

The class roared.

That night, the phone rang. Vonda got up to answer. Vonda answered, listened, and then said, "Okay, we'll work something out."

Back in the bedroom, John asked, "What happened?" "Your brother-in-law is in the hospital with appendicitis."

"Oh wow! That means he'll be down for at least a month. Now I've got four farms to take care of." Vonda asked, "Do you know of anyone that can run his farm?"

"Only Jim. I'll send him up the hill. He can stay there until Don's back on his feet. And also help me as I need him."

The next morning as John and Jim walked to the cow barn, milk buckets in hand. John said, "We had a call last night. Don's in the hospital. As soon as we get our milking done, we'll run up the hill and milk Don's cows and do the chores. You'll have to live up there and run his farm until he's back on his feet."

Jim asked, "I'm not sure what needs to be done."

"I don't know either. After breakfast, we'll look over the farm and figure it out. Hazel is pretty good at knowing what's needed."

At a meeting, John, Hazel, and Jim decided what was to be done. They toured the farm in John's GMC pickup, stopping at cornfields, bean fields, hayfields, and pastures. John said, "It looks like he's way behind in his work. Corn and bean fields need to be walked."

Jim added, "And the weeds in the pasture need mowing." "Yep. Plenty to do. You'll sure be kept busy."

A few days later, John drove up and had a question for Jim. "Did you ever cash that double paycheck?" Jim said, "No, I still have money I brought with me."

"Well, you have to cash the check. Vonda can't keep the books balanced. Get that check!" Jim ran to the house and came back with the check.

John had a rather provocative question for Jim. "Jim, what do you think about me paying you once a year?"

Jim repeated, "Once a year?"

"Yeah. Think about it. If you need money, ask me, and I'll give you what you need and deduct if from your balance due. We'll both keep track, and a couple of weeks before school starts, I'll write you a check for the balance."

Jim pondered the proposal. In less than a minute, he said, "I think that'll work."

Soon, summer was almost over, and there was a bite in the air as John and Jim drove to Avoca. John asked, "How do you feel about going to a new school?"

"I kind of like it mostly because Avoca is a much bigger town than Donia."

When they pulled up in front of Jim's house, John turned to him and said, "Jim, you're a real farmer. You allowed me to do a lot more custom-baling. Have fun in school. I'll be seeing you on the weekends."

Jim grabbed his stuff from the truck and waved to John and headed down the road. John gave a farewell honk on his horn.

Later, Jim was at the Citizens Savings Bank in Avoca. He went in, and as he peered about, a man got up from his desk and greeted him. "May I help you?"

"Yeah. I'd like to open a checking account."

"Okay, follow me to my desk." His nameplate read Jack Ekcan, Customer Service. Jack introduced himself. "I'm Jack Ekcan."

"I'm Jim Pope."

Eckan scrutinized Jim. "Say, are you Bill and Alice Pope's son?" A surprised Jim said, "Yes."

"I know you don't remember me, but your cousin Ponce and I would come out from Council Bluffs to your farm when you lived west of here. We'd spend weekends helping your dad and just fooling around."

"How did Earl get the nickname Ponce?"

"One time we came out to the farm, and your dad asked Earl, 'What do you have on?'" "Earl said, 'I got a new pair of ponce.' From that day on, everyone has called him Ponce.'" Jim laughed aloud.

After the two had enjoyed the exchange, Jack said, "Now let's get down to this high finance. You need to have some money to open a checking account."

Jim pulled some cash and a check from his pocket. "I've got a check for three hundred and twenty- five."

Wide-eyed, Jack said, "That's a lot of money. How old are you?" "I'm sixteen."

"I've never heard of a sixteen-year-old around here with a checking account." Jim said, "I hope to save enough to buy a car."

"I think you've already done that. There's a lot of used cars you can buy for a hundred and twenty-five dollars."

When Jim completed the paperwork, Jack said, "It'll be a couple of weeks before you'll get your checks. If you have a need, you can use what we call a blank counter check." Jack handed him a few checks.

Jim got up, saying, "Thanks, Mr. Eckan. I'll tell Mom I met you."

That Saturday evening, Jim was uptown with his new friends. He said, "What do you do for fun?"

A kid said, "We find someone that'll buy us a case of beer, and we go out on some dirt road and drink it."

Jim rolled his eyes. "You call that fun? Where I work, I can have a beer anytime I want." Another kid said, "Everyone isn't as lucky as you."

Jim said, "I've been on a tractor for two weeks. I'm going to the dance hall and have some real fun." Monday morning in the school hallway, Jim heard someone calling his name. An older boy ran up to him. Jim recognized him. "Hi, Darrel."

"I need help. You know I work at the lumberyard part-time. I also unload freight cars. I have a railcar load of sand that has to be empty by tomorrow. Can you help? I'll split the money with you."

"How long will it take?"

Darrel said, "Until the car is empty. Can you start right after school?"

Jim joined Darrel after school, and soon they were in a bottom dump railcar, scooping sand into the bottom dump. A conveyer belt carried the sand to a berm. Jim said, "We've been at it for two hours, and it looks like we haven't done much."

"Just keep working. When it gets dark, we'll have to rig up a light." Jim checked his watch. "It's almost midnight."

Darrel said, "It looks like we have another two hours or so."

Finally scraping the last of the sand out of the car, Darrel said, "It's three o'clock, made it with five hours to spare."

Jim grinned. "Sleep fast. That's the same time until school starts."

That morning at school, Jim couldn't find Darrel, so he began asking kids if they'd seen him. Jim asked his first-period teacher, "Have you seen Darrel?"

The teacher checked his papers and said, "His mother called. Darrel has an excused absence." Jim returned to his desk and soon was fast asleep.

His teacher shook him awake. "You should go to bed earlier," he admonished.

Jim lifted his hands and, in a groggy response, said, "Sorry, sir, I've been scooping sand until three this morning."

The teacher eyed him. It was obvious he was not lying. "Well, in that case, go back to sleep. I'll give you some homework."

Next day when Jim came in from school, he found a note on the kitchen table. "Go down to the sale barn and see the manager."

In the office, the sales manager said, "I'm told you're pretty good around livestock." Jim grinned. "Yeah, us animals get along."

"Well, if you want it, I have some work for you. I have a farmer bringing in some steers tomorrow for the sale on Friday. He wants someone to stay at the sale barn at night and make rounds checking on his cattle."

Jim said, "Sure. I'll do anything to earn extra money." "Good. If this works out, I'll be calling you again."

Jim was asleep on the couch in the manager 's office when the alarm alerted him that it was time to make his rounds. All went well on that job.

Jim got home from school next afternoon; it was a typical Iowa winter afternoon, snow and ice. When he walked in the door, Alice said, "John called. He wants you to find another boy to help this week-end. He'll pick you up here after school tomorrow."

"With all this snow and ice, what does he expect us to do?"

Alice shrugged. "I guess you'll find out tomorrow. Be sure you have your heavy winter clothes ready." Jim and classmate Elmer Walker found themselves with John in the pickup crawling along the icy road.

He asked, "What are we going to do?"

"I bought six loads of baled hay. We'll haul them over the weekend." "The roads are bad. Think that's a good idea?"

"Got no choice. I'm out of hay. We'll chain up the 88 and you'll pull two hayracks. Elmer will have the H and one hayrack. We'll make one trip tomorrow and one on Sunday. I'll follow along with the pickup in case we have trouble."

"How far do we have to go?"

"It's about four and a half miles."

Jim hated turning out of a warm bed on that cold Saturday morning. Man, it's cold, I don't want to get out of this warm bed. As he dressed, he noticed hand cream and other small bottles on the dresser frozen and broken open. There were little snowdrifts on the inside of the windowsill.

At the breakfast table, Vonda commented, "It's five below zero."

"Yeah," John said, "and with the strong wind, the chill must be fifteen or twenty below. When we leave, I'll go on ahead and make sure everything is ready."

Later, Jim and Elmer, all bundled up, headed down the road with the 88 pulling two empty hayracks and the H pulling one. The chains on the big rear wheels caused the tractor to bounce. Jim thought, better put a saddle on this horse.

It was slow going, but finally, the boys pulled up into a driveway. Leaving the tractors running, they jumped off and ran to the house. A woman was waiting inside the door. She said, "Get in here. You must be freezing."

Pulling a chair close to the stove, she opened the oven door. "Sit here. Take your overshoes and shoes off, and prop your feet on the oven door."

Just then, John stuck his head in the kitchen. Grinning, he said, "What's the matter boys, can't take a little cold?"

Jim, grinning back, said, "I'll flip you to see who drives the 88 r and who drives the pickup home."

John was firm. "You'll do much better with the tractor. When we leave, I'll wait at the bottom of the hill in case something goes wrong. Stay here until you're warm. I'll take the tractors. Hank, his hired man, and I will start loading."

With Jim and Elmer helping, the five of them made short work of loading the three hayracks. But Hank, the hired man, had some reservations. He said, "Jim, I don't know. You'll have a lot of weight pushing you downhill."

Jim said, "I hope the tractor is heavy enough to hold it back." "Yeah, well, it won't take much to break it loose."

John interjected, "I'll wait at the bottom of the hill. There's no through road. You have to stop for the stop sign."

Carefully, Jim pulled the tractor out on the road. At the top of the hill, he stopped and geared the tractor down to first gear.

Crawling down the hill, the weight of the hayracks started pushing the tractor sideways. Jim pushed in on the clutch, letting the tractor coast. As soon as it straightened out, Jim engaged the clutch. Again, the weight started pushing the vehicle sideways, and again, Jim clutched out. The tractor straightened out, and he engaged the clutch. This was repeated three more times before he got to the bottom of the hill. At the bottom, Jim stopped at the stop sign. John was there to meet them. "That was some great tractor-handling! I don't know if I could have done that good."

Jim said, "It was learned as you go."

John, the cold vapor pouring from his mouth, said, "Okay, let's get home and unloaded. The roads are getting better. We'll try to get the other loads this afternoon."

Jim said, "I got that hill pretty well chewed up, shouldn't be any problem later."

Later, they finished unloading the second loads. John heaved a big sigh of relief and said, "Enough work for the weekend. I'll take you home after evening chores."

Jim got home late on Saturday evening. Alice asked, "Only one day's work?"

"We got everything done. We worked outside all day, and I'm frozen through. Don't think I'll ever get warm."

"Well, there's soup on the stove. I'll warm it up." "No thanks Mom, just some hot cocoa."

That night, Jim was shivering even though he was snuggled under a couple of heavy quilts. In the middle of the night, the howling blizzard woke him. He raised his head, listened, and was grateful to snuggle back under the covers.

In the morning, the sound of his mom's voice woke him up. Jim answered, "Yeah, Mom?"

A worried Alice said, "There's a strong wind, and we must have a foot of snow. Would you help Mary with her paper route?"

Jim groaned to himself. "Give me a minute. Are my work clothes dry?" Then he had a major discussion with himself. Worked out in the cold all day. All I want is to stay in bed and get warm. After a while, his moral self admitted, it's family. Gotta do what you gotta do.

It was still dark. Jim and Mary braced themselves against the icy blast. Then with Jim pulling a sled loaded with Sunday papers, they trudged through the snow, the snow having drifted into huge hills in places.

Mary, in a kind of petulant tone, said, "I couldn't have gotten the papers delivered alone." Jim countered, "It's Sunday. The paper is a lot bigger than the weekday paper."

In a while, little Mary admitted, "I'm frozen, Jim."

Trying to boost her stamina, Jim said, "As soon as we're though, we'll go to the mini-mart for cocoa." After what seemed like an agonizing long time in the cold, they were seated at the mini-mart, drinking hot cocoa.

Jim asked, "Are you warm yet?"

Mary timidly asked, "Can I have another cup?"

Jim signaled the waitress by holding up two fingers and pointing at their cups.

The waitress, setting the cups down, said, "What a swell brother you are taking your little sister out for drinks."

Mary, with a big grin, wrapped her cold hands around the cup and smiled.

CHAPTER
FOURTEEN

It was early spring, and the land was once again going through its renaissance of reawakening. Jim was sitting in class. When the period ended, he checked the message board outside the classroom. Seeing one with his name on it, he pulled the note off the board. It read, "Need help unloading a carload of lumber Darrel?"

As Jim walked to the lumberyard, he passed the Schueman Brothers Trucking company. He stopped when he saw a For Sale sign on Diz's 1947 Fleetline Chevy.

Jim went in and was greeted by George Schueman. George said, "Hey, Jim, don't tell me you've got something to haul?"

Jim asked, "Is Diz around?"

"He's out on a job." "How much does he want for his car?" "A hundred and twenty-five."

"Okay, tell Diz I'll buy it."

George asked, "Don't you even want to drive it?" "No, it's okay. I've ridden in it a lot of times."

Jim then pulled a blank check from his billfold, filled it out, and handed it to George. "Give this to Diz." Wide-eyed, George stared at the check. "You have a checking account?" Proudly, Jim said, "It's as good as gold."

The first thing Jim did when he got home was to call Vonda. "Vonda, tell John he doesn't have to pick me up anymore. I have a car." That message too gave him a lot of pride.

On the next school day morning, the kids were milling around the front door, waiting to go in, when Jim pulled up in his new car. Soon his classmates formed a growing knot around the car. One said, "Boy, I wish I had a car."

Jim, joking, said, "First, you have to find someone that will hire you, then you have to save your money. At noon recess, we'll all pile in and go for a ride."

He got a cheer for that idea.

On a weekday evening, Jim and three of his friends were at Nieman's pool hall, shooting pool. When his friend George came in, he said, "Hey, guys, come see what I'm driving."

Everybody rushed outside to get a look at his new Oldsmobile Rocket 88. George readily admitted, "it's Dad's car. Want to take a ride?"

A round of cheers agreed. Soon they were tooling around town, and George said, "Let's get this out on the road and see what it will do."

One kid suggested, "Let's make a speed run to Des Moines!"

Another kid admonished, "It's nine o'clock. We got school tomorrow."

George then said, "It's only about a hundred miles. The speedometer says this car will go a hundred miles per hour. It'll be a good test."

A minute later, they were screeching around corners on the two-lane highway. Suddenly a loud bang told them what everyone knew, the driver 's nemesis: a flat tire. All got out, and George and Jim changed the tire.

Back on the road, they kicked the car up to a hundred miles an hour, and it seemed in no time, they arrived at the Des Moines city limits.

Frank said, "We have to stop and buy something. If we don't have proof we were here, nobody will believe this." So at the next mini-mart, they all bought a souvenir of Des Moines.

One kid said, "Okay, now we have proof."

The others chimed in, "It's after midnight. We had better get started back." George said, "That flat cost us a lot of time. We'll make it up going back." Out on the road, they were halfway home when they heard another loud bang.

Everyone was cussing as they piled out. One kid said, "Now what? My folks will kill me when I get home."

Another said, "We went through a town three or four miles back."

George said, "I can't drive on the rim. Even if I could, what could we do?"

Jim had an idea. "Let's take one of the tires and roll it to the town. Maybe we can find some way to get it fixed."

Jim, Frank and George took turns rolling the flat tire all the way to the town. When they got to the gas station, it was closed.

Frank said, "Maybe there's a number we can call?"

George, getting miffed, said, "Then what? Beg someone to fix it?" Jim piped in, "I've got a check. I'll pay for it."

They made the call and waited. Eventually, a middle-aged man drove up in an old pickup. He said, "So you boys have a problem?"

George pleaded with him, "We have to get back to Avoca. We've been in Des Moines." The man asked, "Do you have a spare?"

George said, "No. We blew a tire on the way."

The man's brows knitted. "And you left there without getting it fixed? Say, you're not the Avoca boys that run all over the country beating up people?"

Frank quickly said, "Heck, no. Those are older guys." The man surveyed the damage. "Do you have money?"

Jim said, "I'll write you a check. Do you have two new tires?" The man shook his head, obviously skeptical. "Yeah."

Jim said, "Mount one, and we'll take the other with us." Soon they were rolling two tires down the road to the car.

The next day at school, everyone was talking about the one-hundred-mile-an-hour speed run to Des Moines. When George arrived driving their farm jeep, everyone flocked around him.

Frank said, "What did your dad say?"

George, grinning, said, "He said if he gets two new tires every time I drive the Olds, I can drive anytime I want."

Frank said, "If Jim hadn't had a checking account, we would've been screwed." It was the last day of school, and Jim and his friends were making summer plans. One said, "I'm gonna work at the mill."

Another 's plans were, "I'm going to help Dad at the store." George asked Jim, "You still working on the farm this summer?" "I'll be there this afternoon in time for evening milking."

Another classmate said, "Save your money. We may need it next year." Jim told him, "Get a job."

Jim was fast asleep in his room at the farm when Vonda banged on his door, calling, "Jim, Jim, something's wrong with John. I have to take him to the hospital!"

Jim jumped out of bed and got dressed.

He found his boss doubled over in pain. Vonda and Jim helped him into the car, and Vonda jumped behind the wheel, calling out, "If I'm not back before the kids wake up, take care of them till I get home."

Back in his room, Jim checked the clock. "It's two fifteen," he mumbled aloud. "This is going to be a short night."

Before the sun was up, Jim was on the phone, talking to Hazel. He explained, "Vonda has taken John to the hospital. As soon as Don is through with his chores, can you come down and watch the kids while I do ours?"

Hazel, as always, was cooperative. "Sure, I'll be down."

Hazel was in the kitchen, drinking coffee. The kids still weren't up when Jim walked in. He said, "Chores done. I'll take over now until Vonda gets home."

Just then Vonda drove in the driveway.

As she entered the kitchen, Hazel asked, "What's wrong with John?" "Appendicitis. He'll be down for three weeks."

Hazel shrugged. "Last year it was Don. This year it's John."

The next day, Jim was cultivating corn when Vonda and the kids drove up in the GMC. Jim drove the H Farmall over, got off, and asked, "Trouble?"

Vonda said, "One of John's big baling customers called saying his hay is ready to be baled." Jim paused then said, "Tell him I'll come over and tie it up."

Vonda said, "But you've never run the baler."

"No, but every time there's a problem with it, I always help John fix it."

Vonda nodded. "Okay, I'll tell him you'll be down in the morning after chores."

Jim said, "I'll leave the tractor and baler there. You'll have to run me back and forth."

Next morning Jim was driving the Oliver 88 and the New Holland baler into Ted Rohn's farmyard. Ted watched as Jim came to a stop, and Ted went to meet him. Ted said, "I was expecting John."

"John's in the hospital. He'll be laid up for about three weeks." Ted cocked his head. "Are you sure you can handle the rig?" "It's a lot smaller than a D-8 Cat."

Still looking concerned, Ted asked, "How old are you?" "Seventeen."

Ted intoned, "Seventeen years old and he trusts you operating this?" Jim simply said, "Where do we start?"

"On the back side of the section. Keep track of the broken bales. " The next day, Jim finished the baling.

Late in the afternoon, Vonda and Ted were talking. Ted handed Vonda a check. "That kid sure surprised us all. You and John have a good hired man."

Vonda grinned and said, "See how fast he matures. You've just changed him from a kid to a man." Ted said, "Next year, there'll be a bidding war for him. How much do you pay him?"

"A hundred and twenty-five a month plus room and board."

Ted's jaw dropped. "A hundred and twenty-five a month! That's what a married man gets!"

Vonda smiled. "He's worth every penny of it, and more. We don't give him the hog and half a beef a married man would get."

One morning after Jim was awakened by his alarm, he dressed in the early dawn darkness and crept past John and Vonda's bedroom. The door was slightly open, and he glanced in. Vonda, sound asleep, was on her back, naked. She moaned in her sleep and raised one leg in a provocative way. Jim gulped and hurried past.

At breakfast, Vonda, at the stove and talking over her shoulder, said, "Jim, was my bedroom door open when you went out?"

Jim kept his eyes on his coffee cup. "I didn't notice." Vonda smirked. "That was the right answer."

CHAPTER FIFTEEN

It was thrashing time. A crew of men were pitching bundles on to hayracks, and other men were pitching bundles into the drag chain of the thrashing machine. Work had stopped for a midmorning break. Some men were sitting in the shade under hayracks, talking. A neighbor 's hired man, Jetta Diea (don't remember his real name; we just always called him by his nickname), was saying, "It seems like a long time ago when we did work with horses."

Another man lamented, "How did we ever get all the work done?" Jetta said to Jim. "Jim, you're lucky. You missed all that."

Laconically, Jim said, "Dad farmed with horses. I helped him all the time." Chuckling, Jetta said, "What could a little kid do with horses?"

Still laconic, Jim said, "I helped harness them. I drove the team while Dad handled the slip scraper." Jetta laughed. "Baloney. I bet you don't know which end to put the collar on."

When John got up, the rest followed. The break was over.

That evening, Jim and John were doing chores. Jim asked, "Could I harness the horse tomorrow and take the team and hayrack out to the thrashing machine?"

John laughed. "You know, I think everyone would enjoy seeing a team harnessed. As soon as the chores are done, we'll get the harness parts together. We'll put a tongue in a grain wagon. Tomorrow I'll send you to the house early before lunch. You can get the horses in the barn and give them some grain. After lunch, while the crew is resting, I'll tell them to come out to the barn."

Next day, after lunch, the men were resting on the lawn. John announced, "Come on down to the barn." The men followed him to the barn where Jim was waiting with the horses in a stall. Jim called, "Okay, you old farts, in case you forgot, I'll show you how to harness a horse." Jim proceeded to harness the team. Everyone watched carefully; most made positive comments. When he was done, Jim leveled his gaze on a quiet Jetta Dia. Jim said, "How's that?"

Jetta said, "I never thought you could do it."

Jim said, "There's probably a lot you don't know about horses. Do you have any idea how Omaha got its name?"

Jetta said, "From the Omaha Indian tribe."

Jim countered. "The way I heard it, the Mormons did it."

Jetta now flared up. "What the hell do the Mormons have to do with Omaha?"

Jim said, "When they were driving a team of horses they used the word gee to tell the team to run right and the word ha to turn left. A woman was driving a team. After she crossed the Missouri River, she yelled, 'Gee!' and the team turned to the right. Her husband, riding on a horse, saw she made a wrong turn and yelled, 'Oh, Ma, ha!'"

The men exploded in laughter, and after they all had had a good laugh, they headed back to work. Jim stayed behind, and when the men were out of sight, he led the team to the grain wagon and hitched them up.

When Jim and the team approached, men stopped work and gathered around, petting and talking to the horses. Tears streamed down their faces.

John finally said, "Jim, better take them back and turn them out."

That evening, John, Vonda, holding Sheila, and Jim were sitting on the porch.

John said, "Tomorrow we'll bale straw."

Jim asked, "How do you bale from a straw stack with a pull-type baler?"

"You just pull it up as close as you can and fork the straw onto the baler pickup." Jim asked, "Don't you have to keep moving the baler?"

"Sure you do, but that's what we have to do. I'll get Don and his hired man to help."

The next day, the four men were pitching straw into the baler. John moved the tractor and baler closer. He said, "Let's take a break and shut the baler engine down."

And all went around to the other side of the straw stack to get in the shade under a hayrack. They were all doing that when Don suddenly yelled, "Fire!"

Flames were climbing, licking in big hungry gulps to the top of the straw stack. The baler and the tractor were already burning. Smoke rose into the sky.

Don jumped on his M Farmall and raced to his house, coming back with a plow. He plowed wide circles around the stack so the fire couldn't spread.

Meanwhile, Hazel had called the fire department. By the time the fire trucks arrived, all that could be done was to keep the fire from spreading.

The Oliver 88 and the New Holland baler were blackened hulks.

When John shut the baler engine down, apparently a hot spark blew out of the exhaust and started the fire.

Neither Jim nor John felt much like talking while they went about their chores. The fire turned out to be a watershed moment for the Kochs.

Next morning, at the breakfast table, John said, "I need to get away from the farm for a while. I'll ship a couple loads of cattle to cover the replacement cost." He turned to his wife. "Vonda, want to take a trip?"

She said, "That would be swell. We haven't been away from the farm since we've been married."

Now John turned to Jim. "Jim, the hard work is behind us. Nothing until we chop corn. Think you can handle the three farms?"

Jim said, "Keep the livestock fed and watered, milk the cows, and don't let the weeds get too high." John grinned. "Spoken like a real farmer."

Vonda added, "Do you think you can take care of yourself for a couple of weeks?" Jim said, "I don't think I'll starve."

Vonda was already full of ideas. "I'll set out the cooking oil and the deep fryer. We got it as a wedding present, but as you know, John doesn't like deep fried food, so it's like new."

John said, "If you need groceries, just put it on our bill. They all know you." Vonda wasn't finished. "I'll prepare some things that will keep in the freezer."

On the day of the trip, Jim helped carry the suitcases out of the house and set them beside the Plymouth. John was busy loading the trunk.

Jim said, "This will be a good road test for the car."

John said, "If I had known I'd be buying a new tractor and baler, I wouldn't have bought it." Jim was comforting. "It's only two or three loads of cattle."

Finally, the Koch family loaded into the car, and they were ready. As Jim shut the door, he got a final order. "Take care of the farms."

Jim, smiling, said, "Keep the shiny side up." He continued to wave good-bye to them until they were out of sight.

Next morning he felt a bit lonely in the empty house. Sure seems cold and lifeless, he was thinking as he picked up the milk buckets from the kitchen counter, where they were left to dry, and he headed for the cow barn.

Jim was in the basement turning the hand crank on the milk separator. When he went into the kitchen, carrying the separator parts, he placed them in the sink, built a fire in the cook stove, and put the kettle of water on it. Pausing, he looked around, deep in thought. Finally, he poured cooking oil in the deep-fat fryer and plugged it in. Soon he was eating fried chicken and french fries. What a breakfast. John, you sure don't know what you're missing.

There was a ditch running through the farm with a large expanse of hemp weeds growing in it. Jim took the H Farmall with two fifty-five-gallon drums mounted on the drawbar and parked alongside the ditch with the motor running and the power takeoff engaged. Then he pulled a long hose with a spray nozzle and walked through the hemp, spraying it.

Who would have guessed that hemp weed would turn into marijuana? I must have killed billion dollars' worth. During World War II the railroad crews were given hemp seed. Has the train moved along the crews scattered the seed by hand. Farmers harvested the hemp and sent it to the Navy to make rope.

That night, the Koch family called Jim from a motel room. John, laughing, said, "Jim, we'll be home around noon tomorrow. Make the girls clean up the house before you kick them out."

"Yeah, sure, I'll tell them. Did you have a good time?"

"The vacation was just what the family needed. I feel like a new man."

The next day, the Plymouth pulled into the driveway. Jim went out to meet them. Noticing all the luggage piled in the backseat, he asked, "Why isn't the luggage in the trunk?"

John said, "Because I have a gold mine in the trunk."

John and Jim went to the rear of the car, and John opened the trunk. Jim was wide-eyed at the load: several cases of beer. An exuberant John said, "This is Coors beer! It's a new brand. It can't be sold in Iowa."

The two stacked the beer on the back porch.

John got in his pickup and made the rounds of the three farms. Jim was anxiously waiting what John would have to say when he returned.

John drove back into the farmyard after making his rounds. Jim was waiting for his report.

"We need to get some of those top enders from the church grounds over here into the dry lot and get them on full feed. Everything looks great."

With that statement from John, I knew John had just given me my farming diploma.

In the kitchen that evening, Vonda was busy preparing supper. John and Jim entered and washed up in the kitchen sink.

Vonda said, "Everything okay with the farm?"

John said, "It's hard with only one tractor. The H just doesn't have the power." Jim said, "And the other person has to do all the hand labor."

John said, "Tomorrow I'll make the rounds of the tractor dealers."

Vonda was busy at the cook stove when baby Bobby went toddling across the kitchen to his mom. He grabbed for Vonda's skirt to balance himself, but he missed, laying the palm of his hand on the side of the stove. His screams filled the room.

Everyone rushed to him. John reached him first. Vonda grabbed the lard can and smeared it on his hand. John sat in the chair, holding the boy, comforting him as he cried uncontrollably, his little body wracked with the sobbing.

Later, Vonda was in the kitchen, holding Bobby on her lap. She unwrapped the bandaged hand and flinched as she saw the big blister covering his palm.

When John and Jim entered the kitchen for lunch, Vonda showed them the blister. She said, "We have to do something."

Everyone put on their thinking caps. John finally said, "I guess we'd better lance it."

Vonda said, "Okay, John, you hold him. I'll hold his hand open. Jim, get a safety pin, and dip the pin in the hot water on the stove."

John held the screaming, squirming Bobby while Vonda pried his hand open and Jim lanced the blister.

A couple of days later, two flatbed trucks drove into the yard. One had a new Oliver 88 diesel tractor. The other had a new New Holland baler. John and Jim rushed out to meet them.

Jim exclaimed, "A diesel! That'll handle three sixteens in road gear." John said, "We needed something with more horsepower."

They watched as the tractor and baler were unloaded. The first thing Jim thought of was, "We don't have any diesel fuel."

John said, "That should be arriving soon."

A while later, a flatbed and pickup arrived at the farmyard. John said, "Mount it beside the gas barrel." The men erected a tall stand and placed a 250-gallon tank on top.

John cautioned "When you fill up the tractors, make darn sure you use the right tank. If you put gas in the 88, you'll ruin the engine."

A few days later, the phone rang, and John answered. He listened and then said, "The price is right, but no more than five hundred head." John then hung up and turned to Jim and Vonda. "That was the Woods Brothers' commission man. He's down in Kansas. He has a chance to buy some draught feeder cattle."

Jim said, "We always have trouble with those underpowered flatland trucks.

John then said, "We make a lot of money off those draught cattle. It's worth losing sleep for."

That night, the phone rang. John got up and answered. Then he went and knocked on Jim's door. "Jim?" "Yeah?"

"First load will be here shortly."

John and Jim were standing beside the 88 when the eighteen-wheeler tried to get up the hill to back into the cattle chute. The driver got out and approached them. He said, "Can't make it up the hill."

So John got on the 88 and backed it up in front of the truck. Jim hooked a log chain to the truck and the tractor. Then John pulled the truck up the hill and stopped while Jim unhooked the chain from the truck, and then the truck backed down to the chute. The cattle were unloaded. John said to the driver, "How many more loads?"

"Six more right behind me, should start rolling in anytime."

As the empty truck pulled away, John looked at his watch. "Might as well do the chores and get the day started. You know what we'll be doing for the next few days."

Jim laughed. "And nights."

CHAPTER
SIXTEEN

It was a hot day. Jim "laying by" (the final cultivating) corn in a field close to the house. He was getting sleepy. Not being able to stay awake, he stopped the tractor, got off, and lay down in the shade of the rear tire and went to sleep.

John calling his name awakened him. "Jim, Jim, you okay?"

Jim woke up looking a bit sheepish. He said, "I'm sorry. I just couldn't keep awake."

"I've done the same thing a few times myself. It's better to take a nap than fall off the tractor. When I heard the tractor engine stop, I thought you had trouble. Go back to sleep."

That night, rain awakened Jim. Hearing it brought a smile to his face. "Rain! No hard work today, too wet."

The next day, it was misty and drizzling by midmorning. John and Jim were waiting in the corncrib for the weather to clear. John said, "Jim, I'm going to be gone for a little while. If the weather clears, go to the pasture and cut weeds."

Jim was soon walking the pasture.

Several days later, Vonda, John, and Jim were in the farmhouse when John said, "Jim, I want you to ride with me."

They got in the pickup and drove off. In a while, they pulled into the farmyard of a farm. Jim looked puzzled. John said, "I bought this farm." With that, they began a tour of the farm. John said, "You can see how neglected it is. Most of the usable land's been in pasture. It'll take a lot of work to make it a productive cropland."

Jim asked, "What about the buildings?"

They looked around. John said, "I don't intend to have any livestock here. Won't need the buildings. I'll clear everything I can to give me more crop room. I'll have a contractor look at the house and maybe rent it."

As they were driving home, John said, "Jim, I know this will be your last year of school and you'll be wanting to get your life started, but would you consider working one more summer and help get the farm productive?"

"Where do you start?"

John said, "Well, all that pastureland has to be plowed. If it gets done before winter sets in, we can plant next spring."

John and Jim were at the kitchen table. Both had papers in front of them. John said, "This is what my figures say I owe you. What does yours say?"

They compared figures.

Jim said, "Mine is the same as yours."

John then wrote out a check and handed it to Jim. John said, "That's your third paycheck." "Yeah. One more to go."

Back at school, Jim heard someone calling his name. It was Alan, who rushed up to him. "Are you going to be able to go to the football game tomorrow night?"

"I don't think so. I gotta work the farm. Lots of fall plowing to get done." Alan, shaking his head, said, "There's more to life than farming."

"A person has to do whatever it takes to survive."

Alan said, "After I graduate, I have to get a job. I don't know what to do."

Jim couldn't resist getting sarcastic. "Well, some of us get to that point sooner than others. Ask your dad to give you a job in his law office." Without more comment, the friends went in separate directions.

Jim worked the new farm on week-ends into late fall. Late Saturday afternoon, he was on the 88 plowing when John drove up in the pickup and waited for him at the end of the field.

Jim stopped and got down, and his boss unloaded four five-gallon cans. "Here's twenty gallons of diesel. I brought you a couple of cheese sandwiches and a pint of milk. That should hold you."

Jim said, "It's a nice, warm evening. I'll plow all night."

"Okay, I'll stop by later tonight when we get back from grocery-shopping."

Jim kept working, his tractor lights showing him the way. Later, John, Vonda, and the kids drove out to the field in the Plymouth. Jim stopped that tractor at the end of the field. John said, "Better call it quits for the night. Leave the tractor, and get in the car."

Jim protested. "I got plenty of fuel. I'm good for the rest of the night." John said, "No, let's go home."

Jim reluctantly got in the car.

Early Sunday morning, Jim got out of bed and was met by a chilly morning. He hurriedly dressed. In the kitchen, John was waiting for him.

Jim said, "What happened to our good weather?"

"Hard freeze."

Jim said, "I don't have any warm clothes." "We'll find something."

John's larger clothes hung on Jim like a scarecrow. He looked rather pathetic.

At the breakfast table, John said, "That's the end of fall plowing. Gotta get the tractor and plow home." Jim said, "A person will freeze to death the way the wind's blowing."

"Well, you bore the brunt last winter hauling hay. I guess it's my turn."

John drove the 88 down the road, pulling the plow. Jim was behind him in the pickup. John parked the tractor in the yard, and both ran into the house to get warm.

The men sat by the cook stove. John said, "Jim, you can have the rest of the winter off. I won't be doing much but tending the livestock after corn-picking is done."

Back in school one day, the cheerleaders were looking for Jim. When they found him, the captain said, "Jim, we got a favor to ask."

"If I'm able."

The captain said, "It's cold, and there's no dressing room at the football field. Could we use your car for a dressing room?" Jim said, "Sure."

"Okay. Park it at the far end of the field in the dark behind the goalpost."

Jim parked the car as instructed and walked away. Six cheerleaders, carrying their uniforms, ran to the car.

At the lunch period next day, Jim and a group of boys were talking.

Charles said, "Now that you won't be working on the farm on weekends until spring, you'll really find out how to have fun."

Bruce, another friend, said, "Now that we have someone with a car, we can go to all these other towns."

Jim asked, "How are you going to help pay for the gas if you don't have money?" One of the boys, Tim, said, "We all get an allowance. We can chip in a little."

Jim said, "What do you do to deserve an allowance?"

Charles had an answer. "Our folks think we should have some spending money." The bell rang, and everybody headed back to class.

Finally, school day was over. Nobody was as exuberant as kids getting out of school at the end of the day. The students poured out of the building in a kind of wild frenzy. A classmate, Delores, ran up to Jim, calling his name.

Jim stopped and waited for her.

She said, "I heard you guys talking during the noon hour. You don't really have to go to the farm on weekends?"

"Not until spring field work."

"Dad is looking for someone to work at his gas station after school and weekends, if you're interested." "Sure, I'm interested. At noon, the guys said there aren't any jobs."

Delores rolled her eyes. "Dad had tried a couple of them. But ..."

Jim said, "If their folks just give them money, why should they work?"

At the Conoco gas station, a week or so later, Jim was cleaning up the service bays. Pete Peterson, the manager, entered the bay and announced, "Let's have a short meeting, guys."

Jim and the two other employees were now standing in front of Pete. "Saturday we're having a sales promotion. We're giving away a pound of lard with the purchase of five gallons of gas. Friday evening Jim will pick up the lard from Skinny Schilling's butcher shop so we'll be ready when we open for business on Saturday. I want everyone here at least a half hour early to help get everything in place before the six a.m. opening."

An employee nicknamed Hot Rod (don't remember his name), said, "Do you really think we'll be that busy on Saturday?"

Jake said, "There's only one way to tell."

Everyone arrived for work early and was shocked at the cars lined up down the block. As soon as men appeared on the station driveway, horns started honking, people shouting for them to get the station open. Pete said, "Jim, get a few cases of lard out by each gas pump. Let's get the station open now!"

All day long, the station was swamped with honking cars urging everyone to hurry. Jim made several more trips to Skinny's for more lard.

CHAPTER SEVENTEEN

Graduation night was here. All the classmates were planning their five-year reunions and saying their final good-byes, pledging their lasting friendship.

On the farm on a rainy day, Jim and John waited in the machine shed, watching the rain. John said, "How about the end of August I let you go?"

There was a bit of sadness in Jim's eyes as he agreed. John said, "You seem sad. You okay with that?"

Jim waxed nostalgic. "Over the four years, I've come to love this farm so much I think of it as my own." "And you show it every day with the care you take with the machinery and the livestock."

"I'll truly miss the family and the farm, but it's a jumping-off place for the rest of my life." "Have you given any thought to what you want to do?"

"Yeah, I have. I want to travel the world and see all the things and places we studied in school. I think I'd like to join the Navy. The submarine service."

Scratching his head, John said, "Isn't that a stretch to go from a farm to a submarine?"

"I had a cousin in the subs during WWII and another one during the Korean War. Hearing them talk about it makes it sound interesting."

Jim stood in front of the Armed Forces Recruiting building. When he entered, he went directly to the Navy section. A man in uniform stood up from his desk and said, "I'm Chief Hobson. Can I help you?" "I just graduated from high school, and I'm thinking about joining the navy."

"Well, son, we have lots of opportunity."

"I'd like to travel, and I've been thinking about the submarine service. I had a couple of cousins in subs. It sounds interesting."

The chief asked, "What kind of background do you have?" "I've been working on a farm for the last four years."

The chief frowned. "Now that's about as far away from the submarine service as you can get. I don't think you'd be a good fit."

"During my seventh through ninth grades in school, our family lived in the janitor 's quarters at the Macedonia School."

"You actually lived in the school building?"

"Yes. We were farming until Dad had health problems and had to find lighter work."

"How were you able to go from farmer to janitor of a school? There are so many safety issues."

"Well, sir, it wasn't easy. All their utility systems blueprints were so far out-of-date they were useless. Dad and I had to trace them out. I drew up new plans, and the school district used them as a guide, drawing up new blueprints."

"You mean you actually hand-traced out all the utility systems and drew up prints?"

"Yes. The electrical system was the hardest. Over the years, subpanels were installed, and the breakers were not marked. Dad had several spells of bad health, and I had to do the work. Dad died when I was in the ninth grade, and I became the janitor."

Chief Hobson said, "I take everything I said back. I think you'd be a very good match for the submarine service. Let's get you tested to make sure you are qualified."

"My last job on the farm will be over the end of August. I want to go to Seattle to see my sister and grandparents, then on to Santa Barbara to see my aunt and uncle."

Chief Hobson said, "Let's go get you qualified for enlistment, and when your traveling is done, you'll be all set to enlist."

At the farmhouse, John, Vonda, and Jim were sitting at the kitchen table. Comparing figures, John said, "They match."

John then wrote out a check and handed it to Jim. "Here's number four. Nobody will believe you worked here for four years and only drew four paychecks."

"I just may not cash this one."

Vonda exclaimed, "No! Don't go screwing up my books. Cash it, or I'll hunt you down."

John now waxed philosophical. "Let's talk about life and the future. How do you compare yourself with others your age?"

Jim thought a while. "I was the only person in our class that had a checking account. Only one other person had a car. A lot of the kids were given money just because their folks felt sorry for them."

"I think that without even realizing it, you've learned a very important lesson. I'm afraid that now that the war and the Depression are behind us, your generation has forgotten the whole concept of sacrifice and self-discipline." Then he smiled, adding, "But you give me hope that things might just work out after all."

The room fell silent as John's words were digested.

Jim rose from the table. "I hear the road calling, folks."

One last wave of good-bye and his 1947 Fleetline Chevy was out of sight.

I did indeed have a great 27 year Navy career serving on five submarines.

USS Menhaden SS 377 FLT ADM NIMITZ FLAGSHIP
USS Halibut SSG(N) 587
HMCS Grilse SS 71
USS Scamp SSN 588
USS Sculpin SSN 590

PHD

My father was a ditch digger
Mother, a clothes washer lady

They toiled everyday preaching to me education was the way
to big pay days and fulfill the dreams so far away.

No matter how I studied,
my dreams were just getting further away.
Working side by side with dad
and studying at night my back aching more each day.

Thrilled, I finely earned my PHD
it was just the tool to get me out of the hole.
Using my PHD kept me above ground where the breezes
were cooling A reward for all that schooling.

My dreams were shattered and felt lower than a beggar
when an employee explained PHD is the Home Depot term for a,
POST HOLE DIGGER.

BY: James Pope

Printed in the United States
by Baker & Taylor Publisher Services